Our April

Our April

A mother and father's heart-breaking story
of the daughter they loved and lost

PAUL AND CORAL JONES

With Geraldine McKelvie

**SIMON &
SCHUSTER**

London · New York · Sydney · Toronto · New Delhi

A CBS COMPANY

First published in Great Britain by Simon & Schuster UK Ltd, 2015
This paperback edition first published in Great Britain by Simon & Schuster UK Ltd, 2016
A CBS COMPANY

1 3 5 7 9 10 8 6 4 2

Simon & Schuster UK Ltd
1st Floor
222 Gray's Inn Road
London WC1X 8HB

www.simonandschuster.co.uk

Simon & Schuster Australia, Sydney
Simon & Schuster India, New Delhi

The author and publishers have made all reasonable efforts
to contact copyright-holders for permission, and apologise
for any omissions or errors in the form of credits given.
Corrections may be made to future printings.

A CIP catalogue record for this book
is available from the British Library

Paperback ISBN: 978-1-4711-3977-2
Ebook ISBN: 978-1-4711-3978-9

Typeset in the UK by M Rules
Printed and bound by CPI Group (UK) Ltd, Croydon, CR0 4YY

For April

CONTENTS

PROLOGUE

In the middle of a leafy, quiet hamlet in mid-Wales, known as Ceinws, the small whitewashed cottage stood apart from the rest of the houses. It sat on a slight hill and smoke had often billowed from the two chimneys on its black, slated roof – a sign that an inviting fire was burning inside. Behind it lay acres of lush green forest and dozens of trees dominated the horizon, their leaves changing colour as the seasons passed.

Once it had been a perfect snapshot of the idyllic life enjoyed by many in the beautiful Welsh countryside. Its name, Mount Pleasant, had always seemed apt.

As the house was five miles from the nearest town, it was remote but peaceful. Its last inhabitant had been a Londoner, an enigmatic man who'd fled the city presumably to escape the ghosts of a past none of his neighbours knew much about.

But on this grey November day, as a sharp chill hung in the air, there was nothing inviting or peaceful about the little white cottage.

For a week it had been barely visible, obscured by the scaffolding that had been built around it, and the trees behind it were bare. The fire had not been lit since images of the cottage had been thrust onto the front of newspapers on that awful day two years previously. Now the chimneys were gone. The black, slated roof had been removed, and only the white walls remained.

The television crews and newspaper photographers had already gathered on the concrete road leading to the cottage when I arrived with my family. We clasped each other's hands as we took our place behind the red barriers. There was a small crowd, some of whom were our friends, others strangers. No one said much, as a handful of workers in high-viz vests buzzed around, making final preparations.

In the front garden there was a yellow crane. As it eventually sprang into life, I could sense my wife's silent tears. Slowly but surely it chipped away at each of the four white walls. One by one they were reduced to rubble.

Less than two hours later it was no more. The house of hell was gone and another chapter in our agonising story was over.

It was comforting to know that no one would ever again have to cast their eyes over that terrible spot, where our lives as we knew them had come to the most horrific end. We still didn't know exactly what had happened on that fateful autumn night in 2012. We suspected that perhaps we never would. All we knew was that it would haunt us until our dying day.

PROLOGUE

We'd come to watch the demolition because we had to see the cottage razed to the ground, brick by brick, with our own eyes. It was only when we surveyed the debris on the ground that we allowed ourselves to hope that the spirit of our beautiful daughter, April, had at long last been set free.

1

A Fighter From the Start

From the moment she was conceived, our daughter April was desperate to live. My wife Coral and I had been trying for a new baby for some time, so when she fell pregnant at the end of the long, hot summer of 2006, we were over the moon.

Our other children, Jazmin, then eleven, and Harley, then five, were just as thrilled as we were and talked excitedly about the arrival of their younger brother or sister. Coral and I knew instinctively that the little life growing inside of her would make our family complete.

'I can't wait to be a big brother!' Harley said almost every day, as he planned the games he'd play with his new brother or sister. 'When will the baby be here?'

Coral and I could only laugh and tell him he had to be patient.

Jazmin was more reserved, but we knew she too couldn't wait for the new arrival.

Looking back on our lives as they were then, it's hard to believe how carefree and uncomplicated our existence was.

Coral and I had first met in 2000, when I was working in my family's hardware shop in the quiet, unassuming town of Machynlleth, where we'd both settled. A sleepy former market dwelling in the shadow of the rolling hills of mid-Wales, it is home to little more than two thousand people. Yet it's a fiercely close community, protective of its own and filled with people willing to go above and beyond for their neighbours. Save the odd Saturday night scrap outside the pub at closing time, crime is virtually unheard of. As we looked forward to April's arrival, it was inconceivable that she could ever come to any harm here.

Coral had grown up in the North Wales port of Holyhead, two hours' drive away on the Isle of Anglesey. Born Coral Smith, she was the second of two children and enjoyed a strong bond with her brother, Ian, who was three years older than her. However, as her sixteenth birthday approached, she was desperate for a taste of independence and began applying for jobs in other parts of Wales. She was intrigued when she noticed a vacancy for a cook in a restaurant in a place called Machynlleth. Reasoning she had nothing to lose, she applied. She was delighted when her application was accepted and, in March 1988, she packed her bags and left her family home behind.

Coral warmed to Machynlleth almost immediately. She made lots of friends and soon she couldn't imagine leaving. Despite the distance, she remained close to her family, particularly her mum, Sue, who visited whenever she could, especially when Jazmin came along a few years later. Likewise, Coral loved her trips back to the picturesque coastal town where she'd grown up. But no matter how fond she was of Holyhead, Machynlleth was now her home.

My journey to the town was somewhat shorter than Coral's, although I arrived there ten years later. I'd spent my childhood in the coastal town of Tywyn, which was just fourteen miles away. I had one younger brother, Philip, known as Fil, and my childhood had been happy. I developed a love of the outdoors as a young child and I was perfectly at home in the beautiful Welsh countryside. Save a brief spell in London as a young man, I could never bring myself to leave.

Like Coral, I'd come to Machynlleth for work when my mum, Lyn, and my stepdad, Dai, had opened a hardware shop and, in 1998, I began to work for them. It was then that my path and Coral's crossed for the first time. She would regularly pop into the shop with Jazmin, then a bright-eyed, sweet toddler, and I fell in love with both of them almost instantly. A feisty, vibrant woman unafraid of speaking her mind, Coral hid a warm, kind heart beneath her tough exterior. She had me captivated and, after a few months of stolen chats, I plucked up the courage to ask her out for a drink.

We had our first date at a local pub and, by the end of the evening, we both knew we'd be together forever. We were soon inseparable and, within six weeks, I'd moved into Coral's home near Machynlleth's iconic town clock. From that moment on I regarded Jazmin as my own.

Two years later Harley came along. But Coral's pregnancy had been fraught with difficulties, culminating in her going into premature labour six weeks before her due date. Harley was in the breech position and eventually had to be delivered by emergency Caesarean. He was also suffering from jaundice. Thankfully they both pulled through and five days later we were allowed to come home.

Jazmin adored her baby brother and we loved family life, but we knew there was room in our home for another child. Coral had some health problems and underwent surgery on her knee when Harley was two, so this prevented us from trying for a baby for a few years, but as we prepared to send Harley to school we both longed to cradle a new-born in our arms again.

Coral realised only a few weeks into her pregnancy that she was expecting. Having already had two children, she recognised the signs immediately and we were both ecstatic when our happy news was confirmed by doctors. But it was soon evident that this pregnancy too was going to be far from plain sailing. Just twenty-four weeks in, Coral began suffering agonising stomach pains. Neither of us wanted to acknowledge the awful reality of the situation, but deep down we both knew she was showing signs of labour.

She was taken to Bronglais General Hospital, seventeen miles away in Aberystwyth, where she was given steroids to stop the labour from progressing.

The next weeks were incredibly stressful, as Coral's labour started again three times. Each time we returned to the hospital, where doctors did all they could to delay our baby's arrival. Overcome by fear for the wellbeing of our unborn child, all we could do was hold each other and will her to fight on.

But the medication given to Coral had terrible side-effects. Soon she was suffering from crippling migraines and was forced to spend entire days in bed with the curtains drawn.

Eventually, in the twenty-seventh week of the pregnancy, we were told we had no choice but to let things progress naturally and hope for the best. The doctors feared it was too dangerous to keep giving Coral steroids, given her reaction to them. We'd already discovered we were having a girl, but our joy was tempered with worry as we willed her to survive.

'Stay strong, little one,' I whispered to Coral's baby bump. The emotion in my voice betrayed the fear I felt for the tiny life inside. I tried to put my faith in the doctors and remind myself that many babies born this early went on to thrive, but it was hard to remain calm when we hadn't been expecting our daughter to arrive for many weeks yet.

A few days later, on 4 April 2007, Coral was in the local bank with Jazmin when a stabbing pain in her stomach told her the time had come for our baby to make her entrance into this world. Ever resourceful and calm under pressure, she finished her business and drove herself to hospital, despite Jazmin's panicked protestations. I hastily arranged childcare for Harley and set out to join them.

By that point we'd become known to the staff at Bronglais and, aware of Coral's medical history, they were keen to transfer her to a specialist hospital across the English border in Liverpool. But, deeply proud of her Welsh heritage, Coral refused.

'I'm having a Welsh baby,' she told them, in no uncertain terms. 'And if you try to take me to Liverpool, I'll handcuff myself to the bed.'

A few hours later it became apparent that April, just like her brother, was in the breech position and doctors told us they would have to perform an emergency Caesarean.

Just a few minutes later, we held our breath as our little girl was taken from Coral's womb. Weighing a tiny 4lb 2oz, she was unable to breathe on her own. I waited for her to let out a cry, but she didn't make a sound as she was placed straight into an incubator.

She was barely the size of a bag of sugar and her skin was almost see-through, with little blue veins visible all over her body. She had a tiny covering of dark hair on her head and, despite everything, I thought she looked beautiful.

'There's our little girl,' I said to Coral, my voice breaking with emotion. 'Our little fighter.'

We both ached to hold our tiny baby in our arms, but knew we had to leave her in the care of the doctors if we wanted her to survive. It was only as Coral was wheeled into recovery that we realised, amidst the chaos of the last few weeks, we hadn't even chosen a name for our daughter. Early on in Coral's pregnancy, we decided on the middle name Sue-Lyn, after both our mothers, but we hadn't had time to think of a first name.

'What about something Welsh?' I suggested. 'Like Seren, for star?'

'There are too many Serens,' Coral replied. 'How about Daisy?'

But no matter what either of us suggested, nothing seemed to stick. After a few minutes of heated discussion, Jazmin had an idea.

'Why don't we call her April?' she said. 'It is the month of April after all.'

Coral and I exchanged a look and, without saying a word, we both knew it was a perfect choice.

'Well, if she doesn't like her name when she's older, she can blame you, Jazz,' Coral replied, woozily, with a smile.

The nurses settled Coral down for the evening and Jazmin and I returned home to Harley. But around 2 a.m., I was woken by a call from Coral.

'They're taking us to Swansea,' she sobbed, panicked. 'They don't think they have the right equipment for April here.'

I quickly found a friend to watch the children and jumped in Coral's car, where I sped back down the windy road to Aberystwyth. I arrived just in time to see Coral and April being taken into separate ambulances.

A doctor explained that April's problems were so complex she had to be treated at a specialist neonatal unit in Singleton Hospital in Swansea, 90 miles away.

'When will I see them again?' I asked, dismayed.

'We don't know,' the doctor replied. 'We want to give April the best care we can.'

All I could do was kiss Coral on the forehead and tell her that I loved her, before I watched the ambulance speed away.

That was the last I saw of Coral and April for the next two weeks. In my early thirties I'd been diagnosed with a rare, degenerative eye condition called Stargardt's Disease. My sight had deteriorated steadily since then. I was perilously close to losing my driving licence and even the short journey from Machynlleth to Aberystwyth was beginning to test me.

Being parted from my new-born baby as she fought for her life was awful, but I knew I could never manage the 180-mile round trip to Swansea, so I focused my attention on supporting Harley and Jazmin instead. They have always been desperately close to their mum and I knew it was tough for them, being separated from her. Despite my worry, I tried my best to put on a brave face for them.

'Your mum and sister will be home soon,' I told them, forcing a smile.

We'd also just moved to a new, bigger home on Machynlleth's close-knit Bryn-y-Gog estate and I wanted to make it as comfortable as possible for Coral and April when they eventually arrived home. I had to convince myself that April would soon be well enough to get out of hospital, so unpacking boxes and doing odd jobs gave me a focus in those first terrifying days.

We'd already decided that April and Harley would share a room for the first few years of April's life, so I set about making it as homely as I could, painting the walls a neutral yellow to stop any arguments when they got older. But the agony of watching your child struggle to live while you can only look on, helpless, is something no parent should have to endure and I wished more than anything I could have been by Coral's side.

Coral recalls:
I didn't really know what was happening when I was woken by the doctors in the early hours of that Thursday morning. I was incredibly weak from surgery. In fact, the pain was so great I couldn't stand by myself. I was bundled into a separate ambulance from my baby and we travelled the 90 miles to Swansea with the sirens blazing. I begged for information about April, but no one could tell me if she was likely to survive.

I hadn't even had the chance to hold April in my arms, but from the moment she'd been taken from my womb I felt an unbelievable rush of love for her, as only a mother can. For almost a month, as the doctors desperately tried to delay her birth, I had spent every day not knowing if she would live or die – and it seemed my nightmare was far from over.

April was taken straight to intensive care, while nurses tried to calm me down and settle me in bed. My body had been through so much, but I couldn't focus on how exhausted I was. Every ounce of energy I had, I spent willing April to pull through.

Over the next few days, I was reassured that the doctors were doing all they could for her. She looked so tiny, so fragile, in her little incubator, but I got through those dark days by reminding myself she was in the best hands. A few days later, I was woken up in the morning to the news she'd suffered a fit overnight, and I was overwhelmed by panic. But doctors had prescribed antibiotics and she'd picked up.

Over the next few days, April continued to fight. Although she'd lost a little weight, her condition had stabilised. I was soon allowed to touch her and feed her and our already unbreakable bond strengthened with every day that passed.

After two weeks, I was told we could take April back to Aberystwyth as she was now breathing comfortably on her own. We were taken to Bronglais by ambulance and shortly afterwards, Paul and the children arrived. I'd never been happier or more relieved to see him.

*

I was overjoyed when Coral called to tell me she and April were returning to Aberystwyth after two long weeks in Swansea. Although we'd had several long phone calls a day, nothing could compare to having our family together again.

But when I laid eyes on April for the first time since I'd been parted from her when she was just hours old, my first feeling was one of panic. At 3lb 12oz, she was even smaller than she'd been when she was born. Although the doctors told us that this was normal, as many babies drop in size after birth, she looked so small she'd fit in the palm of my hand.

In fact, over the next few days, I was so scared of harming her I shied away from picking her up. Instead I simply stood over my tiny daughter's incubator and watched her sleep. Tears welled in my eyes and I felt a mixture of pride and anxiety. We'd nearly lost her so many times, yet each time she'd clung tightly to life, refusing to let go. She was a born fighter.

A few days later we were thrilled when the doctors agreed to let us take April home. As Harley had also been premature, they were confident we'd be able to look after her without assistance. Although I was looking forward to settling into family life, I was also painfully aware of how vulnerable April seemed. She was so small we had to order special tiny nappies for her and a few times I caught myself gazing at her in awe, wondering how someone so little could withstand so much.

I picked Coral and April up at the hospital in Coral's car, but my failing eyesight meant I had to concentrate hard on the drive home. Still a thousand thoughts were racing through my mind and I prayed we'd be able to give April the care she needed. It wasn't until we were in the confines of our new home that I found the courage to pick up my tiny daughter and give her the first of many cuddles we'd share.

Holding her little body in my arms, my heart swelled with pride. In that moment I was sure that the strength of my love for my beautiful baby girl would be enough to protect her from any harm she encountered. I was blissfully unaware of how wrong I was.

2

An Idyllic Childhood

Almost instantly it was impossible for Coral and me to imagine our little home without April in it. While we'd been a happy family of four before she made her grand entrance into the world, we both felt her arrival had completed us. We were the perfect little unit and, far from being jealous of the attention their little sister commanded, Jazmin and Harley surprised us with how much they doted on their younger sibling, always keen to hold and cuddle her. She was so tiny we had to bathe her in one of Coral's mixing bowls, but Jazmin and Harley loved lending a hand.

But April's first year was not without its problems and we were both fiercely protective of our daughter because of the struggles she'd already faced. Coral was determined to breastfeed but her mother's instinct told her something wasn't right, as April would regularly drop off to sleep in the middle of a feed. Although she was aware that all children are different, this worried Coral. Jazmin and Harley hadn't been so easily worn out and she couldn't understand why April always seemed so tired.

Thankfully April was already being closely monitored and, when we received a visit from the midwife a few weeks later, she arranged for her to be seen by a heart specialist. We then made the two and a half hour journey to Alder Hey Children's Hospital in Liverpool, where April was examined.

She underwent various tests and scans and doctors soon explained she'd been born with a hole in her heart. Like most parents, Coral and I didn't have much medical knowledge and were naturally terrified to hear that April had a heart condition and may need an operation.

However, the doctors explained that her condition might not be as serious as we feared, and that there was every chance the problem would correct itself over the next year. Still, April's first year passed in a blur of tests and hospital appointments and her health problems were always foremost in our minds. There was no other treatment that could be prescribed for the problem, so we simply had to wait and hope for the best. Any parent who has been in a similar position will testify as to just how frustrating this can be.

Despite this, April was growing into a bright, beautiful girl and our love for her grew with every day that passed. Blissfully unaware of the battles she faced, she was remarkably contented, with huge brown eyes and a smile that could melt the hardest heart.

She began to meet her milestones and was soon trying to join in our conversations. But, unlike most babies, her first word wasn't 'mum' or 'dad' – Jazmin was thrilled when, instead, she chose to say her sister's name first.

Then, shortly before her first birthday, we were given the good news we were longing for – the hole in her heart had repaired itself naturally, just as the doctors had predicted. The thought of our baby going through major heart surgery was unbearable and it was a massive relief to be told it wasn't necessary for her to have an operation.

We celebrated with a huge party, complete with balloons, toys and party games. Coral had always made a huge fuss of the children on their birthdays and Christmas, but this time she really went all out. Family and friends filled the house and Coral's mum, Sue, made the long journey down from Holyhead. My mum and stepdad, Dai, had given up their hardware shop a few years previously, opting to spend their retirement in the seaside town of New Quay on Cardigan Bay. They now also lived over an hour away by car, but they doted on the children and visited regularly. They wouldn't have missed April's big day for the world.

We'd decided to buy April a rocking horse, but throughout the day our guests added more and more presents to her pile, until there were almost enough new toys and clothes to fill an entire room. Even now, it's hard to look at our favourite photograph of April from that day. Sat at the table in front of her Disney cake, with tufts of curly black hair and a huge smile, she is the picture of innocence and happiness.

As her health improved, she really came into her own. She became a real live wire and she'd climb everywhere – we couldn't take our eyes off her for a second for fear she'd fall and hurt herself, as nothing seemed to scare her. As she grew older and more mobile she began to cause even more mischief – with a little help from Harley, who became her partner in crime. Our hearts would be in our mouths as we'd find them sliding headfirst down the stairs in sleeping bags!

Harley and April also shared a love of the wrestling events which occasionally came to our local community centre. When they heard that one was imminent, they'd look forward to it for weeks, then spend hours afterwards attempting to copy the wrestlers' moves. I'd often be doing my daily press-ups in the living room and, before I knew it, one of them would be jumping from the couch onto my back in a bid to recreate one of the stunts they'd seen. One day, we'd only taken our eyes off April for a second when she managed to clamber up onto a kitchen work surface and knock out half of a baby tooth. This was how she earned the nickname we'd affectionately know her by for the rest of her short life – *diafol*, which means 'little devil' in Welsh.

As much as April could be boisterous, she was also incredibly sweet-natured. By this point, she'd moved from Harley's room into Jazmin's, and Jazz would often wake in the morning to find her little sister had climbed into her bed for a cuddle, accompanied by several of her favourite teddies. She also doted on our two springer spaniels, Autumn and Storm. She was like Coral's little shadow and copied everything her mum did – it wasn't unusual to see her following Coral around with her own little duster while she did the housework, or dipping her hands in the cake mixture as they baked together.

She could also spend hours sitting on our back doorstep, singing little songs she'd made up, usually about rainbows and butterflies, a delightful mesh of English and Welsh words. The neighbours adored her, particularly our good friends Phil and Eirwen who lived next door. They were thrilled when April learned to climb over the small fence which separated our gardens and boldly walked straight into their kitchen. From then on, she'd regularly pop in to see them, armed with a bunch of Eirwen's favourite flowers, sweet peas. When Eirwen passed away in 2010, April felt it keenly. By this point my eyesight had deteriorated so much that I was registered as partially sighted, meaning I was no longer able to work or drive. I'd always led an active, full life and valued my independence, so it was a bitter blow. Coral's numerous health problems meant she too had been unable to take a job for several years and, with three young children to support, money became tighter than ever.

While we didn't have a fancy house, or expensive foreign holidays, there was so much love and laughter in our home that we never felt like we were missing out. With a young family to attend to, our days were far from empty and it was nice to have the time to watch them develop. I quickly found pleasure in the simplest of things and putting April to bed soon became my favourite part of the day. My failing eyes meant I struggled to read her bedtime stories from traditional children's books, so I made up my own. April would squeal with delight as I told her that magical creatures visited her every night while she slept. I insisted that her freckles were kisses from fairies and, if she found a knot in her hair, it was because pixies had been dancing on her head. When she'd finally drift off to sleep, surrounded by teddies, I'd kiss her tenderly on the head and creep back downstairs, so as not to wake her. I treasured our goodnights so much that I dreaded the day she'd become too old to be tucked in by her dad. As I watched my little girl fall into a peaceful sleep, night after night, I had no idea that day would never come.

Sometimes we'd scrape together enough money to take the children on a weekend away, and our trips to the South Wales coast remain some of our favourite memories. Coral and I will also always remember taking April to Drayton Manor theme park in the Midlands when she was a toddler. She was too young to go on any of the rides, but she managed to win a massive dolphin teddy, which was bigger than her. She was so pleased with her prize that Dolphin, as he was simply named, took pride of place in her bed for the rest of her short life.

Shortly after April turned three, we began to notice that she was a little clumsy, often tripping over her little feet. It seemed to affect her more when she was tired, but we were concerned nonetheless, and took her to our GP. After an initial consultation, she was examined by several doctors and a physiotherapist. A diagnosis of mild cerebral palsy was eventually confirmed. We were told this was fairly common in children who have been born prematurely.

April was such a sociable, happy little girl that Coral and I immediately vowed to do everything to ensure her diagnosis wouldn't hold her back. I'd take her for regular walks up our favourite hill, Penrach, which sits on the north side of Machyn-lleth. When she couldn't walk any further I'd pop her on my shoulders and take her to the top. Penrach is a fairly small hill – most of the larger summits would have been too punishing for her, even with my help, but we could still see the whole town stretched out below us as we sat on our favourite white rocks eating oranges and bananas, while I taught her the names of all of the different plants and animals. Bringing up children in such idyllic countryside was a joy and, afterwards, I'd help her pick flowers for Coral before she'd beg me to let her run down a steep grassy verge near the bottom of the hill, as she'd seen Harley do many times.

'Can I try it, Dad?' she'd say. 'Please? I'll be really careful.'

I'd always chuckle and tell her I'd allow her to try it when she was older, knowing her little legs couldn't yet support her. April was determined that she'd one day be strong enough to chase her brother down the hill. The cruel reality, of course, is that she'd never get the chance to try.

Although she could walk for short distances, she suffered from agonising pains on the left side of her body if she pushed herself too far, meaning we still had to use her buggy when she got tired. Sometimes this attracted the odd disapproving glance or snide comment from an ignorant stranger who didn't realise she had a medical condition but, thankfully, April was too young to take any notice. She rarely complained, but at times the pain was so great the thought of climbing the stairs was too much for her, and she'd sit on the bottom step and sob. However, Harley and Jazmin were always on hand to carry their sister to her room.

Despite her problems, April craved the independence her little friends on the estate enjoyed. That's why I couldn't resist buying her a small pink bike when I spied it at a local market shortly after she was diagnosed. It was a simple gift, but you'd have thought I'd handed her the world. I spent hours teaching her how to ride it on the grass outside our house. Her cerebral palsy meant it took her a while to get to grips with it but, after many hours of coaching, she eventually managed to ride it without stabilisers. Soon she pleaded with me to be allowed to cycle to the end of the street. I was apprehensive, and followed closely behind the whole way in case she fell, but I was filled with pride when she managed to get to the last house without any problems.

From then on, you'd rarely see April without her bike. As she couldn't walk far, it gave her a huge sense of freedom, even though she never ventured further than a few hundred yards from the back door. She was thrilled when we bought her a bigger model for her fifth birthday. It too, like most of April's possessions, was pink, which had always been her favourite colour. But her old bike came with such fond memories that neither Coral nor I could face giving it away and it remains with us to this day.

When April was four, she was fitted for a special Lycra suit designed for cerebral palsy sufferers, which doctors hoped would help improve her muscle tone and posture. She was one of the first children in the area to try this treatment, and in a way she was a bit of a guinea pig. When she was being measured for the suit by the manufacturer, she giggled incessantly, telling us that the tape measure was 'tickly'. The manufacturer told us it was a welcome relief, as most children cried the whole way through the process. Of course, we had the suit made in pink and, heavy as it was, she never seemed too upset about having to wear it. We soon noticed a difference, as her balance improved and she became less clumsy.

When it came time for April to start school, Coral and I decided to enrol her in a Welsh-speaking class. Coral has always been extremely patriotic and had already taught April some Welsh words, which frequently made their way into the songs she improvised in the back garden. Her health problems meant we were a bit nervous about how she'd cope with the long school day, but the minute she stepped into her reception class, our fears melted away. April adored school, and when we picked her up at the end of the day she couldn't wait to show us the pictures she'd painted or teach me the new Welsh words she'd learned.

It was around this time that Coral and I made the rather spontaneous decision to get married. Neither of us had ever doubted the other's commitment, but we'd simply never found the time or the money for a wedding. We got engaged quietly at the beginning of 2012. There was no grand proposal, or sparkling engagement ring – we just mutually decided that the time was right. We booked the local registry office for 13 March that year. We thought this was fitting, as it was the twelfth anniversary of our first date. We spent all of our meagre savings on wedding rings and decided that our only guests would be the children. We didn't tell them what we were planning until the morning of the wedding and April shrieked with joy when she was told she'd have another chance to wear the bridesmaid's dress she'd worn at my brother Fil's wedding, two years previously.

The ceremony itself was basic – our witnesses were two members of staff we'd just met in the corridor – but we couldn't have been happier. I'd borrowed some money from my mum so we could have a family meal in the pub afterwards, telling her I was taking Coral out as an anniversary treat. When I phoned her later that evening to tell her we'd got married it took me almost half an hour to persuade her I was telling the truth!

As I put April to bed that evening, she seemed more contented than she'd ever been.

'I'm so glad we're a family now, Dad,' she said. Surrounded by her teddies, her arms around Dolphin, she was struggling to keep her big brown eyes open.

'We've always been a family, sweetheart,' I laughed.

'No, but now we all have the same name,' she replied. 'Mum is a Jones, too. We're a proper family.'

3

1 October 2012

Monday 1 October 2012 began as an unremarkable day. As usual I awoke before anyone else in the house to attend to Autumn and Storm. I let them out about 6.45 a.m. and the weather was overcast with a slight drizzle. I made myself some coffee and soon it was time to wake April and Harley up for school.

I always got April up shortly before 8 a.m. As usual, she was sleeping peacefully surrounded by her teddies. I gently coaxed her awake and, after a few seconds, she opened her eyes and greeted me with a huge smile and a cuddle.

'Morning, honey,' I said. I then took her through to Coral, so she could get her ready for the day ahead. We'd told April that if she wore her special cerebral palsy suit to school, she could take it off when she went out to play in the evenings and she happily accepted this compromise.

While Coral got April washed and dressed and applied the cream used to treat her eczema, it was my job to prepare the breakfast. I made them both a bowl of Ready Brek, with a glass of juice for April and a coffee for Coral. Coral can't abide strong coffee and likes hers to be made in a very specific way – only a quarter of a teaspoon of coffee powder, with three sugars and lots of milk. This meant April liked to steal her mum's cup in the morning and this day was no different. After gulping down half of the sugary coffee, she ate a few mouthfuls of her mum's Ready Brek, too.

'Make sure you leave some for Mum, April,' I said. She simply turned round and gave me a massive cheeky smile, looking like the cat who'd got the cream.

I always did the school run in the morning to allow Coral to get things in order for the day ahead. The school, Ysgol Gynradd Machynlleth, is just a five-minute walk from Bryn-y-Gog and Harley was now old enough to walk with his friends, but April was still too young to make the journey herself. Most days she liked to race me to the gate at the bottom of the garden and that morning was no different. Of course, I deliberately slowed down and she squealed with delight when she beat me.

'I win again, Dad!' she laughed.

When I returned home, I took the dogs on a walk up Penrach. Autumn has always been my favourite season and, feeling the light rain on my face as I climbed the hill, I noticed that the leaves had begun to turn a lovely, deep-red colour. I didn't have much time to spare, as Coral and I had planned to spend the day shopping in Aberystwyth, but I was already looking forward to my next long walk up the hill with April.

Although it was only the beginning of October, we'd started buying a few Christmas presents for the children in a bid to spread the cost a little. Every parent knows how expensive the festive season can be, especially if you have more than one child to buy for. We'd already bought April some clothes and a selection of her favourite Hello Kitty toys, so we'd decided that today we'd look for a television for Harley. We thought this would be a nice surprise for him, as it would mean he could play his Xbox games in his room. Coral drove to Aberystwyth and we spent a few hours mulling over which model to buy, eventually deciding on one from Currys.

By the time we'd paid for the television and bundled it into the car, we hadn't left ourselves much time to get back to Machynlleth for school finishing at 3.20 p.m., so I quickly rang Phil next door and asked if he'd be on standby to fetch April if we weren't back on time.

Fortunately we pulled up outside our house just before the bell sounded and Coral and I headed straight to collect April. As I took her to school in the morning, Coral usually picked her up in the afternoons, but for some reason I decided to accompany my wife that day and I was immediately glad I had. April was so eager to learn and when she told us about what she'd been taught her enthusiasm was infectious. We both loved hearing all about her day.

Looking back, it's hard to find solace in anything that happened on that awful day, but now it seems unthinkable for neither of us to have been there to greet her as she bounded out of the school gates for the final time. April loved Phil and she wouldn't have been fazed to find him waiting for her, but it gives Coral and me the smallest crumb of comfort that we made it back in the nick of time to pick her up ourselves.

At the end of the school day, April's legs were often tired, meaning even the five-minute walk back to our house would test her. On that fateful Monday afternoon I popped her on my shoulders as I often did and carried her home, unaware it would be the last time I'd do so.

'Your hair needs brushing, Dad,' she giggled, running her hands through it, as we walked past the school buses and said goodbye to the teachers. 'It's all messy. I'll do it for you tonight.'

'Thanks, sweetheart,' I laughed. I hadn't had a haircut in a little while and I was aware it was becoming a little overgrown.

'I'm going to put it in a ponytail!' she announced. April loved sitting on the couch, brushing my hair. It was just one of the seemingly mundane tasks which could occupy her for hours as she chattered away, although sometimes she'd mischievously hit me on the head with the hairbrush to make sure I was paying attention.

Sadly April didn't have much time to do my hair that evening, as we had to get back to the school for her parents' evening. Coral and I dropped her at a friend's while we went off to meet her teacher, Mrs Williams.

Mrs Williams was a kind, experienced teacher who had been at the local school for many years. She was loved by all of the children, including April, but on the short walk back to school Coral and I could never have predicted how many people would get to hear about our meeting with her in the coming days. However, as parents, we were privately very proud of the glowing school report April received.

Mrs Williams told us that April had settled in very well since moving up from the reception class. Although she could at times be a bit shy when outside the comfort of our happy home environment, she had lots of little friends and, as the weeks went on, she was becoming more confident about raising her hand to answer questions in class. She also said her Welsh was coming on a treat and she was picking up all the new words she was being taught, which naturally made Coral incredibly proud. April loved art lessons and was never happier than when drawing or making something. Before we left, we were shown some of April's work and we weren't surprised to find she'd painted various pictures of butterflies, which had always been her favourite creatures.

We then returned home and Coral collected April for her swimming lesson. She asked if our friend's daughter could come to the leisure centre with her and Coral agreed. The terrible events which unfolded later that day mean the identity of this little girl is now protected by law, but for the purposes of the story, we'll call her Amy. Amy was two years older than April but they loved playing on their bikes together on the large patch of grass near the front of our house. As she skipped along the road by April's side, this unassuming seven-year-old didn't have a care in the world. In just a few hours, her innocence would be cruelly snatched from her, as she became a key witness in one of the most horrific murder trials our nation has ever witnessed.

By now, Jazmin was seventeen and had left school to study media at college in Aberystwyth. Coral, April and Amy met her as her bus came back into Machynlleth and they headed to the pool together. While they were there, I did some of the household chores and prepared April's favourite dinner, spaghetti hoops on toast.

It was only April's second ever swimming lesson and she was still unable to swim without armbands, but she loved splashing around in the water. When the girls came home, Amy stayed for dinner and they watched the Disney film *Tangled*. April had seen the film once before, but that didn't put her off watching it again. Like lots of young children, when she found a film she liked she'd watch it over and over until she could recite the dialogue off by heart. Her favourite film was the musical *Mamma Mia!*, which she once watched four times in one day!

I was amazed when April polished off the entire plate of spaghetti hoops. Although she loved to steal the occasional bite of her mum's breakfast, her eyes had always been bigger than her stomach and in reality she had a pretty tiny appetite. Getting her to finish her dinner was always a chore and I remember wondering if we'd finally made a breakthrough.

When evening came round, there was an autumn chill in the air but the drizzle had lifted. Soon April and Amy had grown tired of the television and were itching for fresh air.

'Can we please go outside and play?' April asked.

'Yes, but make sure you stick together,' I said.

April and Amy were only outside for a few minutes when they met up with another girl – we'll call her Louise. Louise was in April's class and lived a few hundred yards away. For the next quarter of an hour, the three girls played happily on their bikes together as Coral and I enjoyed a chat with Val, one of our neighbours who had popped round for a visit.

I can say with complete honesty that neither Coral nor I ever had any concerns about April playing outside. We'd check on her regularly, she always respected her carefully set curfews and she knew she wasn't allowed to stray from the boundaries of Bryn-y-Gog. The estate is small – nothing more than a few rows of terraced houses – and, in some ways, is like a big family, where everyone sticks together and looks out for each other. Neighbours are always dropping by for a cup of tea and people are genuinely interested in each other's lives.

One of the reasons our life here was so idyllic was because it felt so safe. We'd never been attracted to city living as it always seemed too busy and dangerous, especially for young children who deserve the freedom to play with their friends without fear. For decades, scores of children have safely played on Bryn-y-Gog's streets, running around and chasing each other on bikes, never far from their parents' sight. There are no main roads and all of the young people are known to their neighbours. Jazmin, Harley and April were always told not to speak to strangers but we naively assumed no one in this tight-knit community could ever do them any wrong. Indeed, before that dreadful October evening, we thought the worst thing that could happen to any of our children here in the heart of the beautiful Welsh countryside was a grazed knee or a punctured bike tyre.

April was never far from the back door and it wasn't long before she and her friends had returned. By now it was just before 7 p.m., and although it wasn't dark the sun had begun to set. The girls tried to bring their bikes through the house and I immediately stopped them.

'You know the rules, April,' I said, firmly. 'Bikes outside, not in the house.'

She took her bike back outside and went into the kitchen to speak to Coral, where she asked if she could play for a little longer.

'Please, Mum,' she said. 'We'll take Louise home and then we'll be right back.'

At the time, allowing April an extra quarter of an hour to play outside seemed so insignificant we barely gave it a second thought. It's a decision parents all over the country no doubt make every night, rarely with any lasting consequences, and Coral figured April deserved a treat because her school report had been so glowing.

'Fifteen minutes,' Coral said firmly. 'But only because you've been so good at school.'

She tenderly zipped up April's purple padded coat before our precious daughter skipped out of the door with her friends and grabbed her beloved bike. She was so happy and full of life that even now it's hard to believe it was the last time we'd see her smiling face.

If only we'd known that in allowing her this small, rare privilege, we had just made the worst decision of our lives.

Unaware of the horror that was about to unfold, we sipped tea and chatted to Val. Around 7.15 p.m., Coral sent Harley to fetch his little sister.

'It's getting cold,' she told him. 'Go and bring April in before it gets dark.'

It's hard to recall exactly how the next ten minutes played out, but one thing we both remember is that we heard Harley before we saw him. His screams were so piercing, so hysterical, that it sounded like he was being tortured. We knew something was terribly wrong and ran to the door to see him racing towards us, gripping the handlebars of April's beloved bike.

A huge knot of dread formed in my stomach as it quickly dawned on me there was no sign of April.

'April's gone!' Harley wailed, sinking to his knees, in what seemed like slow motion. By now, he was almost hyperventilating. 'Someone's taken her!'

In the months following April's disappearance, many people have asked us if we immediately realised the seriousness of the situation. It's true that children can overreact and, statistically, it was highly unlikely that April had been abducted. But from the second I heard Harley's chilling cries I instinctively knew his screams were justified. One look at Coral, whose face had instantly turned ashen, told me she felt the same.

'Oh, God!' Coral cried, eyeing the bike Harley had brought home. 'Someone's got her! Paul, she'd never leave her bike!'

April's new pink bike was, indeed, her pride and joy. She never went out to play without it and we both knew her well enough to appreciate that she'd never abandon it on the street.

Neither of us can remember much about what was said in the seconds that followed, but between sobs Harley managed to tell us that he'd gone to find April when he discovered Amy standing alone and confused on the corner of the street. April's bike was propped up against a garage door across from Louise's house. Amy explained to Harley that April had just got into what Amy thought was a grey car. She told Harley there was a man inside and he'd driven off.

There was no time to waste; we had to phone the police.

Coral recalls:

My hands were shaking as I grabbed the phone. A thousand thoughts should have been racing through my mind but all I could think was that time was not on our side. There are few things more powerful than a mother's instinct and mine told me April was in very real danger.

I could barely breathe as I dialled the number and the operator answered. I knew it was vital to give the police as much information as I could as soon as possible, but every second on the phone was a second spent not looking for April.

'Police emergency?' the voice on the other end said.

I could barely get the words out but somehow I managed to speak.

'Bryn-y-Gog,' I choked. 'Please, my daughter's been kidnapped from Bryn-y-Gog.'

'Hang on a second,' said the operator. 'Tell me again, what did you say, your dog has been kidnapped?'

I felt like I might burst with frustration, but I knew I had to keep calm for April's sake. The signal wasn't the best and I had to make sure the operator understood everything I said. I was vaguely aware of the fact I kept repeating our address over and over, almost as if this would spur someone into action.

'My daughter was out playing with a friend and she's been kidnapped,' I replied. By this point, I was almost hyperventilating.

'You've been kidnapped?' said the operator.

'No!' I wailed. 'My daughter! She's five years old.' I was conscious that I was on the verge of hysteria and I didn't know how much longer I could bear to stay on the line.

'Right, bear with me,' the operator said. 'It's not a very good signal. Are you able to stay still for a moment?'

But in that second, I knew I couldn't stay rooted to the spot any longer. Every minute was precious and there was only one thing I could focus on: finding April. The operator was doing her job as best she could, but at that point it almost seemed irrelevant how long it took the police to arrive. April was my baby. If I couldn't find her, who could?

'No, I've got to go!' I cried, and turned to Val. 'Hang on, can you speak to them please?'

I almost threw the phone in my friend's direction as I sprinted to the door. Paul was pacing up and down the living room and Val was trying her best to keep calm for both of us – although the look in her eyes betrayed the fact she shared our worst fears.

'Hello there, right, can you tell me where you are and exactly what happened?' the operator asked her.

'21 Bryn-y-Gog,' Val said.

'21 Bryn-y-Gog. Where is that?'

'In Machynlleth.'

'In Machynlleth, sorry, I beg your pardon. Right, what makes you think the daughter has been kidnapped?'

In the chaos of the last few minutes, Val suddenly realised how little we knew about what was supposed to have happened.

'What happened, Paul?' she said.

'She's gone off in a car with somebody,' Paul replied, trying desperately not to lose control of his emotions.

'She's gone off in a car with somebody,' Val repeated. 'Some-body's picked her up in a car or something.'

'What is the name of the child who's gone missing?' the operator asked her.

'April Jones,' Val answered.

'April, how old is she?'

'Five.'

'Are you able to describe what she's wearing?'

Luckily Val had seen April when she returned home briefly and was able to describe her outfit in detail.

'She had a white T-shirt,' she replied. 'Black trousers and a purple coat.'

'They haven't got details of the car at all have they?' asked the operator.

At that stage, we didn't know much about the car or the driver. All we had to go on was Amy's description which, amidst the chaos, had been tearfully relayed to us by Harley.

'It's a big grey car with a man driving,' Val said.

'Bear with me, stay on the line for me,' the operator said. By now, I was in the middle of the street, in a state of panic. Neighbours heard the commotion and were gathering in their dozens around the front door, desperate to calm me down and see what they could do to help.

'Everybody's just scattered everywhere to go and look now,' Val said.

'Officers are on their way,' replied the operator.

I began running round the houses, screaming hysterically. I even looked in the bins, just in case April was playing one of her games and hiding from us.

I hazily remember phoning Jazmin, who was at a youth club, and telling her she needed to come home straight away. While

I begged people for information, Paul found Amy and her mum. Between them, they managed to get some information from Amy, who said they'd gone to Louise's, but Louise's dad had told them they couldn't come in as the family was having dinner. A few seconds later, the man had approached them and April had been taken away in what Amy thought was not a car, but a grey van. But there were no vans parked on the estate and we had no more clues as to what had happened.

I have a vague recollection of the first police officer arriving at our house, less than ten minutes after I'd called 999, a kind and calming woman who obviously quickly realised she was dealing with a very serious situation. But I was in such a state of alarm I can't remember anything she said to us.

As soon as you become a mum you feel the most basic need to protect your children. Most parents will understand how terrifying it is to lose sight of your child for a second in a crowded shopping centre, or to see him or her running towards a busy road. But nothing can compare to the horror of having no idea where your child is, or whom they are with. With every second of every minute that ticked by, the terror inside me grew. The pain was indescribable – I felt so consumed by grief and fear that I was sure I would collapse at any moment. The only thing that kept me upright was knowing I had to be reunited with my little girl.

Within fifteen minutes, word of April's disappearance had spread all over Bryn-y-Gog and beyond and volunteers were already congregating on the grass outside our house, combing every corner of the estate and banging on doors begging for information. At that moment in time, I wasn't aware of just how hard all of our friends and neighbours were trying to help find our daughter, but as well as helping with the physical search, they were also furiously uploading April's picture to social media sites, aware that time was very much of the essence. Over the next few months, this amazing sense of community would help sustain Paul and me in our darkest hours.

By now, my already weak knees were in agony and I knew my feet couldn't carry me much further, but the thought of giving up the search was unthinkable. I burst into the house, where Paul was waiting with some police officers. It was only then I realised I was limping badly.

'I can't take this anymore,' I wept. 'I'm going looking for her in the car.'

Panic flashed across Paul's face. 'Coral, no,' he said. 'You can't drive in the state you're in.'

'What do you want me to do?' I sobbed. 'Just stay here and do nothing? Paul, we have to find her.'

'OK, but you can't drive yourself,' he replied. 'I'll get Tim to take you.'

Tim lived a few doors down and was a close friend of Paul's. He was already standing in our garden, eager to do anything he could to help. Like most of the street, he'd come to the door as soon as he heard the news.

'Tim, Coral wants to go out looking in the car,' Paul said. 'Please take her. I can't let her drive, she's too upset.'

'OK,' Tim said.

'I'm going to stay here and wait for news,' Paul went on, handing him our car keys. 'Take her anywhere she wants, just don't let her drive.'

Without hesitation, Tim jumped into the driver's side of our family estate car. A wave of nausea washed over me as I caught sight of April's booster seat and pushchair in the back. I was suddenly gripped by how small and fragile she was. Her little legs would be getting sore and her skin would be hurting without her eczema cream. Oh God, we needed her back.

The countryside surrounding Machynlleth is vast and remote and it was hard to decide where to search first. It was gut-wrenching knowing that April could already be miles ahead of us, in any given direction. To be honest, I can't remember exactly where we went, just that I kept telling Tim to keep driving. Adrenaline and terror coursing through my body, I was desperate for some small clue as to where my precious girl might be. Darkness was setting in and it broke my heart to think of her cold, scared or alone but I had to keep believing she was out there somewhere waiting to be found. I tried to tell myself that she'd soon be back in her room where she belonged, cuddling Dolphin and giggling as Paul made up another of his stories for her.

Tim and I stopped almost everyone we passed. We flagged down other drivers and rolled down our windows to ask pedestrians if they'd seen April, or knew anything that might indicate where she was. Everyone was keen to help but no one had any information.

At one point we were driving along a rural road towards the remote hamlet of Ceinws, when I spotted someone parked just off the main drag. It was little more than an hour since April had gone, but it felt like days had passed. I jumped out of the car and began thumping on the windows. It was only then I realised they had completely steamed up. It didn't take a genius to work out what the people inside were up to. They evidently didn't want to be disturbed but, of course, that was the least of my worries. I banged and banged on the door until the window rolled down and a sheepish-looking young man popped his head out.

'My daughter's missing!' I told him, before quickly describing April and what she'd been wearing. He hadn't seen her – and neither had his female companion – but I wasn't in the mood to take any chances.

At that point, we decided to change direction and head back towards Machynlleth. I can't now remember why we did this, but we had no idea where April was and I was in such a blind panic that I wasn't in a state to carefully plan where we were going.

I had no idea that we'd been less than a mile from the house where my daughter was being held. In my more rational moments, I know that even if we'd reached Ceinws, the chances of us finding April in time to make any real difference were minimal. Ceinws lies less than five miles north of Machynlleth – about a ten-minute drive – and April had already been missing for over an hour. We also didn't have an accurate description of the vehicle or the man who'd been driving it. I don't want to dwell too much on what must have happened in that time, but it's likely my daughter had already come to significant harm. Still, it doesn't make it any less agonising knowing I'd got so close to her so early on in the search.

Tim and I had been driving around for over an hour when I decided to return home to see if there was any news. We'd stopped scores of people and no one knew anything about where April was. I hoped against hope that I'd walk through the back door and she would be there to greet me.

Of course, she wasn't. I sank into Paul's arms and dissolved into tears. I wanted to head straight back out, but a police officer gently suggested it was best if I stay at home and wait for news. I reluctantly accepted her advice. The police were doing everything they could to find April and I needed to preserve my energy, as no one knew what the next few hours had in store for us.

Almost as soon as Coral had gone out looking, I made the decision to stay at home. My vision problems meant I wouldn't be able to provide much help to the others, especially in the fading light. But, more than anything, I couldn't bear the thought of her returning to find both Coral and I had gone. I had to believe she'd be home safe and sound soon, but it was already past her bedtime and she'd no doubt be exhausted and emotional when we got her back.

It was more than I could bear to think of my beautiful girl being scared or in pain. She was such a sweet, funny, loveable child. I couldn't grasp why anyone could ever want to hurt her. Surely, the person who had taken her would just look into those big brown eyes and decide there and then he could never harm her?

Still, it didn't make the waiting around any easier. For the next few hours I paced from the front door to the back door, hoping beyond hope that I'd soon see April walking up the path. Our house was packed with people and the situation began to get very stressful, especially when Coral arrived back home distraught and in need of some space to process what we were dealing with.

Eventually my friend Rich took matters into his own hands and appointed himself as our doorman, only letting close family and friends into our house. We were hugely grateful to each and every person who had joined the search for April, but Rich recognised that having so many people in the house was becoming suffocating for Coral and me.

The police didn't have much information to give us, but at some point in the evening I recall being told that senior officers including Detective Superintendent Andy John, who was leading the case, had agreed Dyfed-Powys Police should issue the UK's first ever nationwide Child Rescue Alert. The system had been used in the USA for many years and was adopted in the UK in 2010, although it hadn't yet been put into practice. It meant that images of April would be circulated to the whole country by the police via the media, so anyone who saw her picture would be on high alert. We'd later discover it had not been an easy decision for the officers to make – as the description of the vehicle April was taken in was very vague. Issuing such a high-profile alert could have risked the investigation team being swamped with information, which could potentially have hindered rather than helped the search, but those involved quickly decided the threat to April was so great that they didn't have much choice. Although the outcome was not as we'd hoped, we will always be grateful to them for making this difficult decision in such stressful circumstances.

By now there were hundreds of people looking for April and I had to keep believing there was a chance we might find her. Jazmin had gathered a group of friends and they were knocking on doors all over the town, asking anyone they could find if they knew anything. We told ourselves that someone, somewhere, must know something.

When your child goes missing, your concept of time is turned completely on its head. Every second without them seems like an eternity, yet you're desperate to stop the clock because the chances of finding him or her safe and well diminish with each hour that passes. I didn't know much about child abductions, because these things simply didn't happen in Machynlleth, but I'd read in the papers that the first twenty-four hours were crucial.

By the time 10 p.m. came round, I was still frantically pacing from the front gate to the back. I felt so helpless, yet the idea of sitting down even for a second made me feel unbearably guilty. April had been gone for less than three hours and I was still telling myself she'd walk through the door at any moment.

That's when I experienced it – a horrible sensation like nothing I've ever felt before. I've never been much of a believer in anything mystical, and I'm deeply sceptical of anyone who claims to have a sixth sense, but as I stood at the front door a horrible chill came over me. It's hard to explain, but I instantly felt sick to my stomach and I was suddenly aware that there was now a huge hole in my life that could never be filled. It was almost like I could feel all sense of hope leaving my body, no matter how hard I tried to cling on to it. Don't ask me why, but in the space of a second I just knew April wouldn't be coming home that night.

I tried to fight the feeling but, deep down, I think I already knew the awful truth. My little girl was gone forever.

4

The Search

By the early hours of Tuesday morning exhaustion was etched on Coral's face, so I suggested she get some sleep. She was desperate to feel close to April, so she climbed into her bed and nodded off for an hour or so, cuddling some of her beloved teddies, which still had her scent on them.

There wasn't much we could do but sit and wait for news. The police had set up roadblocks and were stopping all motorists leaving Machynlleth, handing them leaflets with April's picture on in case they'd seen anything. Specially trained dogs were also searching the town for clues.

I was certain I'd never sleep, so I stayed in the living room while Coral went upstairs. A few friends volunteered to keep us company. Rich stayed by the door and Coral's friends, Mel and Melere, said they would stay the night, too.

We spent most of the night in silence, glued to the 24-hour news channels. The Child Rescue Alert had instantly seen the coverage of April's disappearance evolve from speculation on social networking sites to headline news, and Dyfed-Powys Police released a statement saying officers were increasingly concerned for our daughter's welfare. I tried hard to focus but one hour just merged into the next. I must have been getting tired, but I didn't notice. I couldn't sit still so I paced around the house. At one point I suddenly became aware of how hungry and thirsty I was and I went to the kitchen to grab a biscuit and make a quick coffee. It was only when I looked at the clock I realised it was 4 a.m.

Coral had barely been asleep for an hour when she came back downstairs.

'Any news?' she asked, hopefully.

'Sorry, love,' I said, taking her hand in mine. 'Nothing yet.'

As night gradually turned into morning, we huddled together on the couch and watched the news reports, which were playing on a loop. We hardly noticed dawn breaking. Overnight hundreds of volunteers had congregated at the local leisure centre to help search for April. Some had travelled over 100 miles in the dead of night to be here, from all corners of Wales and parts of England. Pubs in the town had emptied as people took to the streets to look for our daughter, some staying out all night. The local petrol station had remained open through the early hours to deal with the huge influx of vehicles which needed to be fuelled, with workers graciously agreeing to do overtime. We were overwhelmed by their kindness.

Around 11 a.m., the officers who had been with us through the small hours were relieved and two others arrived. They introduced themselves as Detective Constable Dave Roberts and Detective Sergeant Hayley Heard and told us they were our family liaison officers – or FLOs for short.

Hayley spoke first – she was caring, yet a little more reserved than Dave, an affable extrovert with a strong Birmingham accent. He soon took over and, without invitation, pulled up a chair and planted himself in the middle of the living room floor. Coral and I were so fraught we didn't grasp much of what he was saying and I remember him repeating himself a lot.

'Hayley and I are now your first point of contact,' he said. 'We'll be with you for the duration of the case.'

Dave took control of the situation with such ease but Coral and I were so vulnerable that we didn't realise how vital this was. It almost makes me laugh now to think I mistook his professionalism for cockiness. I've often wondered if Dave and Hayley knew how profound an effect this investigation would have on their own lives, as they sat in our living room for the first time on that Tuesday morning.

Dave later told us he'd been getting ready for work as normal around 7 a.m. when his phone had begun vibrating with a call from the station in Aberystwyth. He now admits it was a conversation which changed his life forever.

'You need to get into work now,' a senior officer said as soon as he answered, wasting no time on pleasantries. 'A five-year-old girl has gone missing in Machynlleth. It's a suspected abduction.'

Dave agreed to come in at once, but he was sceptical at first. It was early in the morning and he hadn't turned his television on, so he hadn't seen the headlines. Even in sleepy mid-Wales, the police dealt with countless missing children every week. Some had stayed too long at a friend's house and some were even at the centre of bitter custody battles, a pawn in a battle between warring parents. They always turned up. Children weren't abducted in Machynlleth, not in the true sense of the word.

'Dave,' the senior officer said, before she rang off. 'This is real.'

Those three, simple words sent a shiver down Dave's spine. He threw on his coat and jumped in his car, driving as fast as he could from his home in the remote Ceredigion countryside to Aberystwyth. He had no idea what role he would be asked to play in the investigation. It was only when he got to the station that he was told he would be one of two family liaison officers.

This was where he was introduced to Hayley for the first time. They'd served in the same force for many years, and it was incredible that their paths had never crossed, but they'd never been put on the same case and, as a result, had no preconceived ideas about each other. They were briefed as thoroughly as possible on the previous night's events, but there was no time to waste and they had to get to Machynlleth as soon as they could. On the relatively short journey through the Dyfi Valley that morning, they had to get to know each other very quickly.

We didn't know what to expect when, startled and exhausted, we opened the door to Dave and Hayley, but over the next few months they would be towers of strength for our family. Looking back, it's difficult to imagine how we would have coped without them. We didn't know it then, but we'd just met two people who would prove to be loyal friends long after the investigation had finished. At some points they would almost become part of the family, putting their own lives on hold to be by our sides through the worst ordeal any parent can imagine.

While our FLOs were introducing themselves to us, the police were holding a press conference. It was vital that as many people as possible were looking for April and, in that respect, we were thankful that news of her disappearance had fast become the leading story on every channel and was spreading like wildfire on social media. Several television presenters, including Davina McCall and Phillip Schofield, had also appealed for anyone with information to contact the police. We weren't immediately aware that the media had begun congregating on Bryn-y-Gog, but more and more reporters and photographers would arrive over the course of the next few hours.

It was around then that the name Mark Bridger first came up. Early that morning, Amy had been interviewed by a police officer specially trained in speaking to child witnesses, who established that the van she described may have been a 4×4-type vehicle. Amy also told the officer that April had got in the driver's side. She had then been given pictures of various vehicles in a bid to get more information about the driver who had taken April. One of the cards showed a Land Rover Discovery identical to Mark Bridger's and she'd picked it out straight away.

We'd been watching the news for so long and we'd seen all the reports so many times that they were barely registering with us. But, once the interview with Amy had been carried out, new footage of Detective Superintendent Reg Bevan briefing reporters in Aberystwyth was being shown.

DS Bevan said that police had some new information on the vehicle. He had to choose his words carefully, as they were working on the observations of a vulnerable little girl, but he suggested April could have been taken in a Land Rover – though it was what he said next that caught our attention.

'The witnesses have told us April got into the driver's side,' he said. 'It may well be that she got in with the driver but, of course, that could mean it's a left-hand-drive vehicle.'

Coral and I looked at each other, each knowing exactly what the other was thinking. 'Bridger,' we both said, immediately.

Although we later discovered that Bridger had already become a person of interest to the investigation, none of the police officers in the house had mentioned his name to us yet, as the information they had on him was still very sensitive. But Machynlleth is a small town and he was the only person we knew who owned a left-hand-drive car, which just happened to be a grey Land Rover Discovery. We weren't yet aware that a witness had seen him in his car on the estate around the time April vanished. This wasn't remarkable in itself, as several of his children lived there, but in light of the information from Amy it would prove to be a key sighting.

'At least we've got something,' I said to Coral, trying to convince myself as much as anyone that this was a positive development. 'We know something. That's good.'

At that moment we were so focused on finding April that Mark Bridger was almost irrelevant. We didn't yet feel any anger towards him – all we wanted was for him to give us our daughter back and we were clinging desperately to anything that might tell us where she was. I was so numb and exhausted I'd almost become incapable of feeling anything.

As it was the only emotion I remember experiencing at that point was shock at the fact that April had apparently been taken by a local. Perhaps because the concept of a child being abducted was so alien to me, I assumed April had been taken by a faceless stranger passing through the town – a loner in an anonymous van, with no ties to anyone we knew.

Over the next few weeks and months, reports in the press would contain various accounts of our relationship with Mark Bridger. Some suggested that he was a close friend of mine, others that we even thought of him as family. These were all wild exaggerations. In truth, I hadn't had a proper conversation with Mark Bridger in years. He had dated the sister of a former girl-friend of mine in the late nineties, but we were rarely in each other's company. We'd nod to each other on the street and per-haps we'd say a few words – nothing more than that.

At forty six, he was just a few years older than me and had lived near us when we'd first moved to Bryn-y-Gog. Shortly afterwards he'd broken up with his long-term partner and since then he'd stayed in various places in the area. A father himself, he had six children to numerous different women, and I'd heard on the grapevine that he'd just become a grandfather. Long before April was born, he'd had a few games of darts with Coral in one of the pubs in the town and it would later emerge that he'd sent Jazmin a friend request on Facebook shortly before April vanished. Jazmin had no connection to Bridger and when she asked him why he had sent her the request, he claimed it was because of these tenuous links to our family.

All this considered, I wouldn't say April knew him as such. It would probably be more accurate to say she knew of him, as

Harley sometimes played with two of his children, who were neighbours of ours. He often drove to the estate to pick them up and she'd likely have recognised his car.

Still, it seemed inconceivable that he could be responsible for taking her but there was no time to waste – we had to tell Dave and Hayley about our suspicions.

'We think you're looking for a man called Mark Bridger,' I said. 'He's the only person in Mach with a left-hand drive.'

Dave and Hayley sprang into action straight away and began asking questions of the friends and neighbours who were gathered in the house. Bridger had recently moved from his address in Machynlleth to a rented cottage in the village of Ceinws, near where Coral and Tim had been searching the previous evening. Ironically the house was called Mount Pleasant. Now, it's impossible to distinguish fact from rumour, as there is so much speculation about his behaviour in the weeks before April was taken, but we've heard on the grapevine that he had specifically sought a property with a fireplace.

However, the police were unaware of his change of address and, as a result, had broken down the door of an innocent man who had just moved into his old house. Thankfully it isn't easy to stay hidden for long in a community like ours.

'I think I know where he is,' Mel told Dave. 'I think he's moved to Ceinws.'

Dave immediately relayed this information to senior officers at the station. Unknown to us, the man accused of taking our daughter had begun feigning concern for her wellbeing. In the early afternoon he had joined the search, telling other volunteers he'd been out all night looking for her. Several of them thought his behaviour was odd. In particular they were struck by how clean he was for a man who'd allegedly spent hours roaming the countryside. The volunteers were unaware that the police were hot on Mark Bridger's heels.

Officers took off to track Bridger down. They located his cottage and forced entry into the house, but he'd already gone. The property was uncomfortably hot and they immediately noticed an overpowering smell of detergent – but there was no sign of April. It was becoming increasingly obvious to them that this was a man with a lot to hide. Half an hour later, they found him walking on the A487, the main road between Ceinws and Machynlleth. He was arrested and taken to the police station in Aberystwyth, where officers started questioning him in connection with April's abduction.

We weren't aware of these developments until several hours later. Dave and Hayley were keen to keep us in the loop, but they were also anxious not to give us false hope or to relay any information before it had been confirmed. Emotionally we were hanging by a thread and it wouldn't help to bombard us with information before the police could be sure it was accurate.

In the meantime, we had to give the police some of April's belongings so they had samples of her DNA. This could prove vital if officers needed to verify any sightings of her. It broke our hearts to hand over her hairbrush, toothbrush, mug and some of the teddies from her room. I couldn't bear to give them Dolphin, so I chose a few others but made the police promise we'd get them back. Swabs were also taken from Coral, Jazmin, Harley and me.

It wasn't until evening time that Dave told us we would shortly receive a visit from DS Andy John, who had some important news. By now, detectives had spent many hours quizzing Bridger. Although I still hoped for the best, I think I'd already begun to prepare myself for the worst.

We asked the majority of people in the house to leave, only allowing close family to stay. It was at that point I realised Harley was playing outside with a group of friends, one of whom was one was Bridger's son. It was the most surreal of situations.

'Probably best if they go home,' Dave said, gently.

Andy John arrived shortly afterwards, around 8 p.m. He was a tall, thin man with steely grey hair. He had a sympathetic manner, which made both Coral and me warm to him almost immediately, but the expression on his face told us he wasn't here to give us good news. Dai, my mum and Fil were allowed to remain in the house but they had to stay in another room while we were briefed. Only Dave and Hayley could be by our sides.

As soon as we were seated, Andy started to speak.

'There's no easy way to say this,' he began, carefully, as I squeezed Coral's hand. 'But we've got Mark Bridger.'

I'd suspected this would be the first thing he'd tell us, but it didn't stop my stomach from lurching as beads of cold sweat prickled my neck.

'He has made a statement saying he killed April Jones on the evening of October 1st, 2012.'

I instinctively wrapped my arms around Coral but I don't think either of us had started to cry yet.

'He said he was driving his car down the road when he felt a small knock,' Andy went on. 'He got out and realised he had hit April. In a panic, he put her in the Land Rover Discovery and drove around Machynlleth not knowing what to do. He tried to revive her by giving her mouth to mouth but failed. He then can't remember what he had done or where the body was placed.'

I felt shock cascade through my veins as I held Coral tightly. Both of us found it hard to speak, but we needed to hear more.

'We're not sure we believe his account of what happened,' Andy said. He explained that there appeared to be no blood on the road, or on the car, although they'd have to wait for a forensic report to confirm this.

'Do you think there's any chance she's still alive?' I heard myself asking, my voice finally breaking, as I clutched at straws.

Of course we wanted to believe that April wasn't dead, but I hadn't been able to shake off the horrible feeling I'd had the previous evening, that sense of foreboding that my worst fears had come true. It was a few seconds before Andy spoke, but it felt like an eternity.

'We're still pursuing various lines of inquiry but I think it's bad news if he's saying she's already dead,' he eventually replied, meeting my eye. 'I'm so sorry.'

It had been agreed that some of the news could be relayed to the rest of the family if they promised not to divulge what they knew, as the investigation was at such a crucial stage. The next few minutes passed in a blur of tears and chaos as the awful news was broken to them.

Our life as we knew it had been shattered into a thousand pieces but I was almost oblivious to the sobs ringing out around me. All I knew was that our old world had ended and a new world had begun.

*

When Andy left that evening, we were visited by a doctor who gave Coral and me some diazepam to help us sleep. It was the last thing I wanted to do, but Dave and Hayley reminded me I needed to keep my strength up. As I climbed into bed, I suddenly realised that my body was aching with tiredness but my mind was still racing. But a little while later the pills kicked in and I fell into a deep, dreamless sleep. I managed just short of six hours before I woke up and was hit instantly by a wave of nausea. Opening my eyes, it hit me all over again – April was gone. How could I have slept when my little girl was lost? I had to rest, but I felt sick with guilt.

The next morning, Coral was desperate to do anything to help the police get answers and they suggested we could do a television appeal.

Coral recalls:

For most normal people, the idea of going in front of the nation's media at the most vulnerable point in their lives would be terrifying. I can't deny I was scared, but the nerves paled into insignificance compared to my fears for April. I was clinging to any tiny shred of hope I could that my baby was still alive. While there was still no body, I couldn't give up hope and I prayed that the television appeal might trigger a vital clue.

It was hard for Paul and me to grasp anything at that point, but we were vaguely aware of how much interest there was in April's story. I hadn't really left the house since the night April vanished, but friends told me that by the hour more and more press were gathering on the estate. Most were camped out less than a hundred yards from the house, armed with cameras, microphones and notepads. One brazen photographer climbed our fence and trampled all over the flower garden as he tried to take a picture of the house, but he was quickly chased away by the police.

We decided that Paul would remain at home while I took part in the press conference. I desperately wanted him by my side, but we agreed that Jazmin and Harley needed his support. However, the thought of doing the appeal alone was over-whelming so I asked Dai to come with me.

The police took us to the council offices in Aberystwyth, as the police station wasn't big enough to accommodate the media. It was only two days since I'd last made this journey, but I felt like a different person from the woman who'd been excit-edly browsing for her children's Christmas presents. This time it was a blur and I could barely see through my tears. I could tell Dai was trying his hardest to be strong for me, but his own pain was written all over his face. April was the apple of his eye and she'd always rush to greet him with a huge hug whenever she visited.

Hayley introduced me to the police press manager, Rhian Davies-Moore, and Detective Superintendent Reg Bevan, who had spoken at the previous day's press conference and would now be appealing for more information. Rhian and Hayley then helped me draft my short statement and it was agreed that Dai would read it for me if I became too emotional to con-tinue. They told me to keep drinking water in case I became too warm under the heat of television lights, but my own wel-fare was the last thing on my mind. I was relieved when they told me not to answer any questions from reporters – just getting through my statement would be hard enough.

It was only when I walked into the room where the press were gathered that I realised how big a deal the appeal was. It was the first time either Paul or I had spoken directly to the media and they'd turned out in their droves. I'm not sure exactly how many people were there, but it seemed like hundreds. As soon as they caught sight of me, the room became a sea of flashbulbs and everyone seemed determined to thrust a camera or a microphone in my face. It all seemed so ridiculous and unfair – I should have been getting ready to pick April up from school. It was hard to believe that two days ago I'd been a normal mum.

I was led to a table, where I was sat with Hayley and Dai on one side and DS Bevan on the other. Behind me were some of our most treasured pictures of April, along with a headshot of Bridger and a photograph of his car. Just displaying April's picture next to that of her suspected abductor seemed criminal, but it was essential that as many people as possible saw our little girl's face. We'd picked two of the most recent pictures we could find – in one she was wearing one of her favourite pink dresses and the other showed her sitting on a wall dressed in the padded purple coat she had on the night she was taken. It was painful that what had once been private family photographs were now public property, splashed across the front page of every newspaper in Britain, but I'd have given up every picture I owned if it led us to April.

As I started to speak, a hush descended on the room and I wanted to curl up in a corner and cry, but I knew what I had to do for my daughter.

'It's been thirty-six hours since April was taken from us,' I began, trying my hardest to keep the sobs at bay. 'There must be someone out there who knows where she is and can help the police find her.'

Now the cameras and microphones were edging closer. As reporters and photographers elbowed each other out of the way to get nearer to me, it felt like a pack of wild animals was descending on me and I was powerless to stop the attack. I'd been warned by Hayley and Rhian that this might happen, but nothing could have prepared me for how daunting it was. With the benefit of hindsight, I can appreciate that everyone in the room had a job to do, and the support of the media was vital in helping spread the word about April's disappearance, but for an ordinary person who has never asked for any kind of fame or publicity, this kind of attention is truly petrifying, especially when you are already at your most fragile. Somehow I found the strength to keep speaking.

'We are desperate for news,' I went on, aware that my voice was shaking more and more with every word. 'Please, please help find her.'

As soon as I said the last word of my statement, I couldn't stop the tears. I'd forced myself to say what I had to for April before I dissolved into sobs. I was vaguely aware of DS Bevan placing a supportive hand on my arm. It was a small gesture, but comforting nonetheless. For the rest of the press conference, I sat with my head in my hands, weeping uncontrollably as Dai tried his best to console me. Thankfully, Bevan was able to pick up where I'd left off.

'In relation to this specific investigation we are pursuing a number of lines of inquiry and Mark Bridger is one of them,' he told the room. By now, I was crying so hard I could barely breathe.

'In relation to the images I circulated to you earlier today, which was the Land Rover Discovery and Mark Bridger's photograph, can I again ask, did you see this vehicle between Monday evening and Tuesday afternoon? Do you know Mark Bridger and did you see him during that period, between Monday evening and Tuesday afternoon? If you have any information please contact us on the Child Rescue Alert Line.

'Do not assume somebody else has already contacted us with information. Even if you feel yours is trivial, it may be the vital piece that we are missing.'

I was ushered away as reporters barked questions at me. I can't remember much of the journey home, but as I walked through the front door it hit me all over again – April wasn't here. Although there were dozens of people trickling in and out of the house, it seemed so quiet and morbid without my daughter's infectious laughter. Her toys were still strewn across the floor and her teddies tucked up in her bed. It was so hard to believe she was gone.

Overnight I'd become obsessively protective over anything belonging to my daughter. If anyone touched her favourite biscuits, I'd be on the verge of a meltdown. I even burst into tears when someone tried to use a carrier bag she'd had at school a few days before she vanished.

I was given some more sleeping tablets that evening and I managed to doze off for a few hours, but every time I opened my eyes my grief hit me like a ton of bricks and tears began to stream down my face. Paul tried his best to comfort me, but his own pain was ripping him apart.

I'm not sure how either of us managed to get up the next morning, but somehow we did. We were desperate to maintain a shred of normality for Jazmin and Harley, who didn't realise just how bleak things were looking. Harley's teacher kindly agreed to collect him and take him to school to get him out of the house for a few hours.

Dave and Hayley came round shortly after 9 a.m., but they didn't have much news for us. For Paul and me the waiting around was torture. By now, there were almost 400 people looking for April, but we were asked by the police not to join the massive search party. There was such intense press interest in the case that they worried our presence would attract unwanted attention, which could harm the chances of finding April.

It felt unnatural, sitting at home while volunteers from all over the country braved the wind and rain to help the police and mountain rescue team look for our little girl. But we had to put our trust in the police. At the end of the day they knew best and we had to do what was right for April.

But I felt like I might explode with frustration if I spent another minute sitting around. April had been missing for over two days and I desperately wanted to do something, anything that might help bring her home to me. At that point, I'd convinced myself there was a chance she could still be alive. That's when I came up with the idea of making pink bows. Pink had always been her favourite colour and I thought it would be a nice way of keeping her at the forefront of everyone's minds.

Making the bows gave me a focus. Within hours, friends had rallied round to help and a shop in the town had kindly donated some pink material. Over the next day, word of the pink bows spread and people started making their own. It wasn't long before almost every house in Bryn-y-Gog had a pink bow tied to its gate. Shopkeepers soon caught on, displaying them in their windows, and a giant pink bow was tied to the railings at the town clock. I was overwhelmed by how quickly the bows had become a symbol of hope for April.

I also wanted to show my gratitude to the volunteers. We had some spare tins of biscuits lying around, so Melere gave me a lift to the community centre to drop them off. It was the least we could do. Luckily, we used a lesser-known side entrance and managed to avoid being detected by the press.

By the Thursday, our house was still packed with friends and family and the press were camped outside, so our FLOs had decided that it was no longer sensible to share sensitive information about the investigation with us in our own home.

Dave and Hayley quickly realised that our little terraced house was the centre of our family life. It was the only place April had ever lived and we'd made so many happy memories with her there. They appreciated that in the weeks and months ahead, it would be important for us to keep those memories intact, as far as we were able. As officers with over fifty years of service between them, they knew only too well what kinds of awful things the police might have to share with us as the investigation progressed.

Unbeknown to us, they'd been working hard behind the scenes to provide a 'sanctuary' for us – a safe house at a secret location where we could speak to officers in private, away from the prying eyes of the press. This would also double as an office for Dave and Hayley. As grateful as we were for the support of our family, friends and neighbours, from early on the police made it clear to us that anything they told us must be treated in the strictest confidence or we risked prejudicing the investigation.

At first, Dave and Hayley had tried to find a room for us at the small police station in Machynlleth. However, as this was the most high profile case the police in our small town had ever dealt with, it had become a hive of activity overnight and as a result was incredibly chaotic – even the rest room would have been too busy to accommodate us. Dave then began ringing round local businesses and eventually found one which had a spare room. Of course the room was completely bare, and Dave thought it looked too clinical, so he'd spent most of Wednesday evening making it look homely – sourcing tables, chairs, some plants and a fridge. He hung photographs he had taken of local landscapes and wildlife on the wall to make it look as welcoming as possible. It's hard to describe how much of a difference these little things made.

Our first meeting with Andy John at the sanctuary came late on Thursday afternoon, when Dave and Hayley received a phone call from him asking if he could meet us. Bridger was still in custody and forensic teams had been working round the clock, combing his cottage and his car for evidence which might help lead us to April. Dave and Hayley knew there had been an important development, but they didn't know what it was.

By this point, the press had realised that Dave and Hayley were our FLOs and whenever they were seen coming in or out of the house, rumours of developments in the case started to circulate amongst them. To us, it was important they didn't find out where the sanctuary was. After updates on the case were delivered, it was crucial we were given time and space to process what we'd been told and it certainly wouldn't help if we were besieged by photographers at the front door.

Dave and Hayley picked us up at the house and drove us there, where Andy was waiting. It was only a short journey – around five minutes in the car – but Dave kept his eye on the rear-view mirror at all times, in case an eagle-eyed photographer spotted us and tried to follow. Thankfully no one seemed to have noticed us leave the house.

The mood was sombre. It was hard for Coral and me to know what to feel. Given what we'd been told on Tuesday evening, it was obvious that the police were working on the assumption April was dead. If Mark Bridger had killed our daughter, we wanted them to uncover every scrap of evidence they could find so we had the greatest chance possible of putting him behind bars for the rest of his life. But the more evidence they found, the more our already slim hopes of finding April alive would crumble. Coral, in particular, was finding it extremely difficult to accept our daughter was gone. Like any mother would be, she was still full of hope that we were being summoned to the sanctuary because April had been found safe and well.

But, as soon as we stepped into the place, we knew the news wouldn't be good. Andy had the same grim expression on his face as when we'd first met him on Tuesday. There was little point in formalities and we were both glad when he got straight to the point.

'The forensic teams have identified spots of April's blood in Mark Bridger's house,' he said, slowly. 'We're confident this means that April was in the house.'

I nodded, willing him to continue.

'We also believe this means she came to significant harm within the property,' he added.

Neither of us said much. I'm not sure if we even cried. A thousand questions were running through our minds, but we didn't have the strength to voice them.

I'd expected to be hysterical but instead I felt like something was clawing at my insides and slowly destroying me, bit by bit. What had that bastard done to my little girl?

Andy didn't stay long. He knew that we'd already built up a strong rapport with Dave and Hayley and it was better if we talked things through with them. They spent the next few hours explaining the implications of this development to us. The forensic team had used the samples of April's DNA taken from the belongings we'd handed over to establish that the blood did, in fact, belong to her. Even though there was no sign of her body, the investigation was fast becoming a murder inquiry.

'Is there any way it's not April's blood?' Coral asked.

Dave bowed his head. 'The results of the DNA profiling show that it is,' he replied. 'The chances of these results being wrong are around one in a billion.'

Early the next morning, Bridger was arrested on suspicion of murder. We were told the police had until 5 p.m. that afternoon to formally charge him. We knew this was coming, but it didn't make it any easier to hear that awful word.

At times like this, it's easy to slip into denial. While I'd accepted what the police had told us the previous evening, when the tears finally took hold of me in the early hours I began to allow myself to doubt what they'd said. Perhaps April was still being hidden somewhere and the spots of blood in the cottage had appeared because she'd grazed her knee or cut her finger? Plus, there was no sign of her, dead or alive. How could the police know anything for sure?

But, realistically, we knew they were now looking for a body – and all we could do was wait.

We didn't attend the press conference held by the police that morning. Although she would have done anything to help find April, Coral had found Wednesday's experience very distressing and there was no real need for us to face the cameras again.

However, the news channels were still playing in the living room as friends and family made endless cups of tea and coffee, desperate to help but not sure what to do or say. Detective Superintendent Bevan, along with another senior officer, Superintendent Ian John, briefed the media on the latest developments, both wearing pink bows.

Perhaps most significantly, they announced that the search was to be scaled down and that the hundreds of volunteers who had turned up to help find April were no longer required. From now on, the search would be carried out solely by professionals.

Superintendent John told reporters: 'We want to acknowledge and are extremely grateful for the efforts of the community volunteers who have supported the professional searchers in trying to locate April. They have been a vital part of our team throughout this search operation. Quite frankly, their commitment has been an inspiration to us all.

'The dynamics of the search have now changed and, due to the passage of time and the developments within the investigation, it is no longer appropriate for us to expect untrained members of the public to continue the search.

'Now, we only require professional searchers to be involved in the ongoing search which continues in and around Machynlleth.'

Afternoon came and went but there was still no sign of Bridger being charged. We were soon told that the police had been granted special permission by the court in Aberystwyth to hold him for another twenty-four hours of questioning.

It was a very trying time. While Coral and I knew about the damning forensic evidence, we couldn't share these details with anyone – not even our closest family. Dave and Hayley impressed upon us just how important it was to keep this information to ourselves, as neither the search team nor even many of the officers assigned to the case knew about the development. If it was leaked, it could significantly harm the investigation. In fact, if and when the case came to court, Bridger's lawyer could argue it had affected his right to a fair trial, particularly if the media printed details of the evidence before it had been put before a jury. As much as it pained us to keep things from the people who had provided such unwavering support to us, we knew we couldn't breathe a word of what we knew to anyone.

Dave and Hayley explained that in many cases where a child has been murdered, some key evidence has actually been withheld from the parents until the trial because the police have been so concerned that they might, even unwittingly, share some sensitive information with someone who shouldn't be party to it. In our case, Dave and Hayley told Andy how important it was for us to kept in the loop and how we could be trusted to keep details of the evidence to ourselves. Dave stressed that there was only one condition attached – neither of us could be told anything unless the other was there. If one knew something the other didn't, not only would this cause confusion, which could potentially harm the investigation, it could also fuel resentment between Coral and me.

That night, reporters on television reminded viewers that if Mark Bridger had not been charged by 5 p.m. the next day, officers would have no choice but to let him walk free. To Coral and me, this was nothing short of unthinkable.

'They need to speed things up,' I said to Dave. I was trying to keep my cool, but anger had now started to set in and I was powerless to stop the rage that was mounting against the animal who had taken my precious girl. The idea of him walking away without so much as a slap on the wrists made me feel physically sick. 'They can't just let him go!'

After spending hours in the pressure cooker that had become our home, you could have forgiven Dave if he'd lost his temper from time to time, but even on this most testing of days he remained as calm as ever, no matter how anxious he was inside.

'Paul, that won't happen,' he told me firmly. 'Let me tell you, he's going nowhere.'

I didn't know what to believe and I was barely aware of darkness falling. I'm not sure if either Coral or I slept at all, but when we got up the next morning all we could think about was the 5 p.m. deadline and the prospect of the man who appeared to have taken April being released. A long day of agony stretched out ahead of us as we waited to hear his fate.

Fortunately Dave recognised how distressing this was for us and decided that he and Hayley should take us out for the afternoon.

'Why don't we go down and have a look at the pink bows?' he suggested.

The idea of going anywhere or doing anything that wasn't essential seemed ridiculous, but Coral and I were beginning to feel suffocated in the confines of the house. Everywhere we looked there was some reminder of April and, although we were grateful for all of the support we'd received, the living room and kitchen were constantly packed with people. We barely had room to collect our thoughts.

I felt a lump spring up in my throat when we were driven down the main street in Machynlleth: there wasn't a window or a fence post which didn't have something pink on display. As well as bows, people had put out teddy bears and balloons in April's favourite colour. These were such simple gestures but they gave us an idea of just how many hearts had been broken by our personal tragedy. Machynlleth had been rocked to its core and would never be the same again.

While we were driving, Dave noticed some members of the mountain rescue team who had been out searching in the town and pointed them out to us.

'I'd love to shake their hands,' I said.

Dave immediately pulled over. 'Do you want to shake their hands?' he asked.

I looked at Coral and we both nodded our heads. 'Yes,' we said, in unison. We hadn't realised this was a possibility but we were desperate to say thanks to the people who'd braved the elements to search for April round the clock.

'Well, why don't we?' Dave said.

Hayley then got out of the car and stopped the searchers in their tracks.

'Mr and Mrs Jones would like to speak to you,' she said.

We couldn't express our gratitude in words, so we simply grabbed hold of their hands and said a simple 'Thank you.' All of them had tears in their eyes.

By coincidence, Dave and Hayley met two members of the team the following evening, as they were staying in the same hotel, a few miles outside of Machynlleth. They later told us that there were more tears as they recounted the meeting and Dave joked that the searchers were speaking as if they'd met the Pope. It took us just a few minutes to thank them for their work, but I don't think we'll ever truly know how much it meant to them.

The police promised us that we'd be the first to know of any developments. Dave and Hayley knew we'd been glued to our television for the past few days and the last thing they wanted was for us to hear it on the news. We'd initially been told Andy wanted to meet us at noon, so we couldn't stray far from the town, but the meeting was postponed several times. This didn't do anything for our nerves. It was important Dave and Hayley had mobile phone reception to allow them to speak to Andy whenever he called, so Dave then drove us up one of the hills on the south side of Machynlleth. He told us to spend a few moments together, while he and Hayley waited in the car.

From early on, it was clear that our relationship was important to Dave. He knew how much we needed each other, but he
was also painfully aware of how the murder of a much-loved
child can rip even the strongest of marriages apart. I've heard
varying statistics on the issue, but it's believed fewer than ten per
cent of couples will stay together after experiencing this kind of
trauma.

It was only then Coral and I realised we hadn't had any time
alone together since April was taken. Those precious few moments, where we could cry together and console each other,
provided a little comfort, albeit small. Although it would be push-
ing it to say we enjoyed ourselves – with April gone, we felt like
we'd never, ever enjoy anything again – the fresh air and serenity
of the countryside did give us a sense of relief. While the whole
country appeared to be rallying round us, no one in the world felt
the loss of April as keenly as we did.

In that moment, I spontaneously removed a pink ribbon from
my pocket and tied it to a fence post. In the coming weeks and
months, I'd climb this hill many times to do the same thing. It
would become a daily pilgrimage and soon I had tied over eighty
pink bows to that same post.

A few minutes later, we were interrupted by Dave, who'd got
out of the car and was rushing towards us.

'We need to go,' he said. 'Andy is heading to the sanctuary
now.'

With no time to waste, we got back into the car and Dave drove
us back into the town. Andy had already arrived at the sanctuary
by the time we got there.

'We've had the go-ahead from the Crown Prosecution Service,' he said. 'Mark Bridger has been charged with murder, abduction and attempting to pervert the course of justice.'

Andy reassured us that the search teams were still focused on finding April. Tears sprang to Coral's eyes, but my first feeling was one of relief. I was just so glad Bridger was off the streets and that we would get our day in court. Naively I assumed this meant we'd soon find out exactly what he did with April.

But, over the next few hours, reality began to set in. Our friends and family were still gathered in our living room, anxious for news. A breakdown in communication between the Crown Prosecution Service and the police meant the news was released to the media before Dave had a chance to update them and we returned home to a very tearful group of people. It was only then I began to process that the charges were confirmation of the unthinkable. April was dead.

It was difficult to imagine feeling any worse than we did. In fact, the agony was only beginning.

5

The Evidence

Two days after Mark Bridger was charged, he appeared in court in Aberystwyth. Neither Coral nor I felt strong enough to attend, so we watched the coverage on television at home with Dave and Hayley. It was only a five-minute hearing, and the television cameras were not allowed in the courtroom, but the scenes outside when Bridger arrived were quite something.

Huge crowds had amassed and they were obviously baying for his blood. None of those gathered got to see him, as he was driven into court in a van behind a police escort, but several had to be restrained by the police. Others stood at the side of the road and hurled insults at the van as it passed. It was a strange feeling – we felt sorry for the police, who had to control the crowds, but it was hard to feel any anger towards the people who'd turned out. Most of them would be parents and grandparents themselves and this was their worst nightmare. Compared to what Bridger had done, this paled into insignificance.

The Monday also marked a week since April had been taken and, emotionally, we were on the edge. In the space of seven days, our lives had become unrecognisable.

The previous morning, there had been a procession in April's name, followed by a vigil at St Peter's Church in Machynlleth. Around 700 people had walked through the town, most wearing pink bows. Coral and I had made the last-minute decision to join the walk, although we shied away from going to the church, as we knew we were likely to be spotted by the media there. It was a stressful experience for Dave and Hayley, as we only told them of our plans around fifteen minutes beforehand. Given the intense press interest, significantly more police officers would have been on duty had they known in advance that we wanted to be there. But, ever calm under pressure, Dave managed to get us a last-minute police escort and warned all of our friends to let him know immediately if they saw any reporters or photographers. A huge group of neighbours formed what we like to call the 'ring of steel' around us. At one point, Coral was close to collapse and had to be supported by her friend Tracey and me. Together, we carried her through the crowds. It was an overwhelming experience but, as the streets were so packed, the press didn't see us. At one point, I even walked past a man with a huge camera and he seemed to take no notice of me.

We didn't want the Monday to be dominated by Bridger's court appearance – we had to make it about April. There is a scene in *Tangled* where two of the characters are singing to each other on a boat when the sky suddenly fills with Chinese lanterns. April loved this part and she was in awe of the lanterns. As this was the last film she watched, it was hard for us to remember it without becoming tearful. But the thought of sitting in the house, waiting for the clock to strike seven and replaying the previous week's events was agonising, so Coral had the idea of releasing some of our own lanterns for April.

'If she's still out there somewhere, they'll guide her home,' she said, hopefully, though both of us knew the hope was gone.

Friends and family helped us source as many lanterns as possible and soon there were none left in either Machynlleth or Aberystwyth. Others also came with balloons. By early evening, the grass outside our house was packed with family, friends and neighbours, whose lives had been touched by April. At 7 p.m., we released them and, for a few minutes, they gave the dusky October sky a beautiful orange glow. It was a bittersweet moment.

Now Bridger had been charged, all we could do was wait for the trial, but it was impossible for us to return to any sort of normality. A few weeks later, the local council agreed to light up the clock tower in pink as a tribute to April, and Dave and Hayley offered to take us out to see it. As we were preparing to leave, I suddenly remembered what day it was – 22 October, my 44th birthday. Without April, the day was meaningless. Even now, I'm not convinced I'll ever feel like celebrating my birthday again.

In those first few weeks, Coral and I developed very different ways of coping. I began exercising to the point where it was almost excessive, regularly running for five or six miles or spending hours in the gym. I'd barely go a day without trekking up the hill Dave and Hayley had taken us to the day Bridger was charged, my pockets full of pink ribbons. Some days, I'd find myself climbing it twice. Once, I got to the top and realised I'd forgotten the ribbons so I went straight home to get some and climbed the hill again. Punishing myself physically felt like a release, but even then I had a terrible sense of guilt at having almost enjoyed something. With Autumn and Storm at my side, I'd sit on a rock and look down on the town below, which had once held so many happy memories for me. Lost in my tears, I'd sometimes be oblivious to the fact hours had passed.

One afternoon, I was walking alone with the dogs when I turned round to see two people following me. They looked familiar and I soon realised I recognised them – they were news reporters who'd camped out on Bryn-y-Gog when April first went missing. I wasn't sure what publication they worked for, but I didn't care. While I'd never have suggested that the press shouldn't report on April's story, my walks up the hill were one of the few things that provided me with any comfort and I was enraged that these private moments should be violated. My family had never asked to be in the news and I didn't want to become public property. I turned round and shot the reporters a look and, without a word, they turned and left. I worried that they might try and follow me every day after that, but they never attempted it again.

Coral, on the other hand, was broken. For someone who'd once been so active, spending her days volunteering in the school, baking cakes with the children and driving everyone around, she became like a shell. Overnight the feisty woman I'd fallen in love with had gone from living life to the full to merely existing. Weight began to drop off her and soon she'd lost over two stone.

She lost interest in eating, and some days she'd survive on a couple of mouthfuls of Ready Brek. In the first week or so, she'd barely been able to sleep at all and was relying on tablets from the doctor to get some rest. But as the weeks wore on, the tables turned completely and she began staying in bed for sixteen hours a day. Often, she'd come downstairs and lie on the couch for a few hours in the afternoon before going straight back upstairs. It seemed that the only way she could cope with the massive burden of grief was to draw the curtains and shut out the outside world.

It was around this time that Hayley suggested I begin keeping a diary. Not only would this help keep track of important details, she also thought it might be cathartic to write about my feelings. I was a little unsure at first. As well as my poor eyesight, I suffer from dyslexia, so writing can be a bit of a challenge. But as soon as I started putting my thoughts down on paper, I felt some kind of release. Tears filled my eyes as I started to think of what I'd say to April if she could hear me.

'April, you leave a hole so big in me it may never be fixed,' I wrote. 'I'm only glad I had as much time with you as I did. It looked like it may have been less when you were born. Five and a half years of so much love. I can't explain to anyone what it means to me.

'Love you, Dad xxx.'

When I'd finished these first few sentences, the tears had spilled out of my eyes and down my cheeks. From then on, I vowed to write in the diary every day.

But as I began to collect my thoughts, some of them became dark. I imagined April's little body lying in a ditch or a shallow grave, or dumped down a mineshaft as if she were an animal. I was so tortured by the images in my head that I thought about writing to Bridger and begging him to tell us where she was, but I couldn't bring myself to waste my words on him when I could devote them all to April.

One thing that did bring us some comfort was the beautiful pink bows which adorned Machynlleth, a reminder that April was still in everyone's hearts. However, both Coral and I knew that there would come a day when they would be taken down so the town could move on.

It was then we had the idea of having pink bows tattooed on our hands as a tribute to April. We liked the idea of making the bows permanent in some way and having them on our hands would make us feel like she was always with us.

We booked an appointment at El Diablo Tattoos in Machynlleth. The tattoo artist was a friendly and professional man who called himself Rambo. It was obvious he recognised us straight away but he treated us very sensitively and he was careful not to pry.

We both blinked back tears as he got to work on us. I'd decided to have the words 'love you' inked next to my pink bow and Coral chose '*gobaith*', the Welsh word for hope. The sitting took a few hours, but we were delighted with the results. It was a bittersweet moment as the tattoos were beautiful but, of course, we wished we'd never had to have them done in the first place.

April had been gone for around a month when Coral decided she needed to drive again. She'd spent so long in bed that she didn't have time to go out, and she hadn't been in the car since she and Tim had been out searching. Naturally she'd been avoiding it, as it now held such painful memories, but Coral's car was a lifeline.

Because of her knee problems, she could never walk far, but like April and her bike, she loved the independence it gave her.

'If I don't get back in the car now, I never will,' she said.

There was just one thing we had to do first. April's car seat and buggy were still in the back of the car.

'Paul, please put them in the attic,' Coral choked. We couldn't contemplate throwing them out, but neither could we live with such painful reminders of the perfect life we had before the nightmare had begun.

As soon as I caught sight of my daughter's things lying undisturbed, I couldn't stop the tears. How could she be gone? We had hoped that one day soon her legs would be strong enough that she wouldn't need her buggy. Now I couldn't bear to think of never having the chance to wheel her around in it again.

I carried the buggy and the car seat into the kitchen and Coral immediately broke down. I thought her heart might break in that moment. As I held her to me, I realised my own tears had turned into choking, guttural sobs. In the end, neither of us had the strength to open the attic, so Jazmin volunteered to do it, though it was easy to see the huge tears glistening in her eyes, too. After we'd carefully placed April's things inside, we closed the door and virtually collapsed with grief. None of us was able to do anything else for the rest of the day.

Dave and Hayley had promised to keep us in the loop as far as possible and they stuck to their word. We were soon told that Bridger's trial would be likely to take place in February and that it would last around a month. At first I was adamant I could never sit through it. At that stage we had almost no idea what had happened to April, or what we were likely to hear. From early on in the case, it became obvious that the police we working on the assumption that she'd been sexually abused before she died. I expected I'd have to sit for weeks on end, listening to details of all the horrible, sick things that monster did to my little girl and I convinced myself I'd never cope.

However, Coral was adamant she wanted to face our daughter's abductor in court and I knew I couldn't let her do it alone. Given what we'd have to go through in the coming months, statistically the odds were already stacked against our marriage, and Dave emphasised how important it was for us to do things together if we wanted to do what was best for our relationship. Life without each other was unimaginable – we had to take his advice.

Dave and Hayley also told us that, as far as they were able, the police would share the evidence with us before the trial, so we could process it in our own time before we had to face Bridger in court. This reassured me slightly, but it didn't stop the familiar feeling of dread when, around a month after April's disappearance, we were summoned to the sanctuary for a meeting with Andy John. Dave and Hayley drove us there and the mood was bleak.

'We have some more information from the forensic teams,' Andy said. We knew this wasn't going to be positive.

'What have they found?' I asked, taking Coral's hand in mine.

'They discovered there were traces of a substantial puddle of April's blood on Mark Bridger's living room floor. There were also spots of blood in the hall and in the bathroom.'

'What do you think this means?' I asked Dave.

'I'm afraid if you'd lost that amount of blood, I don't think you'd get up again,' he replied. 'I'm sorry, Paul.'

It was confirmation of what we already knew, but it didn't make it any easier to hear.

That night, I went upstairs and shut myself in Harley's room, where I cried solidly for six hours. I didn't think it was possible, but I shed so many tears I was in physical pain and my eyes, cheeks and jawbone ached. I don't think the awful reality – that April was gone forever – had sunk in until now. As the evidence against Bridger mounted up, the situation was becoming unbearable.

Coral and I have always been very much in tune with each other's feelings, to the extent we can almost tell what the other is thinking. I think this is why, even in the darkest moments, we rarely broke down at the same time. Perhaps we knew that one of us always had to try and stay strong for the children. The next day, however, was a different story for Coral. The new information hit her like a ton of bricks and she spent most of the day crying in bed, while I looked after the children.

It didn't help that everything we did reminded us of April. As she'd needed a little more support than her brother and sister, we hadn't realised how much our lives revolved around her. For me, evening times were the worst. Not only was this the time that she was taken, it was the time when we shared our most precious moments as I put her to bed. Harley and Jazmin were too old to be tucked in or to listen to my fairy stories. In an attempt to fill the massive void, I'd spend the evenings writing in my diary instead.

'Her bed is now made up with quilts and blankets,' I wrote. 'Pillows and teddies all round – just no April. We've known for a long time that she will never fill that bed again. I'd give my life for one more goodnight.'

While some days we wanted to do nothing more than lock ourselves in the house with our grief, there were so many things to do from a practical point of view. We were advised by the police that the trial would take place at the Crown Court in either Mold or Caernarfon. Both were around an hour and a half from Machynlleth by car and the judge decided, in the circumstances, that he'd let Coral and me decide which building we'd prefer. Dave and Hayley arranged to take us to see both courts at the start of November to help us make a decision.

We immediately felt uneasy in Caernarfon. As soon as we arrived, the security guard insisted on thoroughly searching us both. He went through every individual item in Coral's bag, which made her very distressed, and made no apology when he saw how upset we got. We understood that these checks were important, but for two very fragile people the manner in which they were carried out was humiliating and made us feel like criminals and not victims. Dave had some very stern words with the security guard and we can only hope he has now learned to be more sensitive with grieving families.

To add to this, the courtroom made Coral feel claustrophobic, as it was very cramped. Since April had been taken she'd become extremely anxious when faced with big crowds. If we chose to have the trial there, we'd have to walk through the whole court to get to our seats at the front. This doesn't sound like a big deal, but it was a daunting prospect as we knew there would be hundreds of people packed into the small room, including dozens of reporters. We also wouldn't have been able to see Bridger from where we were seated. This was especially important to Coral as she wanted to look him in the eye and force him to see the pain on our faces.

We were then driven to Mold, which was around an hour away. Although we were searched going in, it was nothing like our experience in Caernarfon and the staff were much more sympathetic. We were also told they could arrange for us to have our own private room in another wing of the court, and there was a side entrance which would allow us to go straight to our seats without walking through the whole courtroom. It wasn't a hard decision to make and we told Dave and Hayley almost straight away that we preferred Mold.

Dave and Hayley took us to McDonald's for lunch. Coral and I were both a bit withdrawn before I explained that we'd taken April here a few months previously, on our last visit to Holyhead. They were very apologetic and said we could go somewhere else if we liked, but we told them not to worry. It just seemed that everywhere we turned there was a reminder of April. As we drove home, we passed through lots of estates like ours in lots of different towns, with children like ours playing on the streets. I couldn't help but wonder, why us? I'd never have wished the pain we were feeling on my worst enemy, but it seemed so unfair that this burden had somehow landed on our shoulders. What were the odds of our April being taken? It must have been thousands, if not millions, to one.

Things got even worse as Christmas edged closer. Jazmin and Harley were remarkably resilient but we knew the whole situation was taking its toll on them and we wanted to at least have some kind of Christmas for them.

Coral recalls:

I'd always been good at budgeting for Christmas – buying things throughout the year so I could spread the cost, so I already had quite a lot of gifts for the children. Knowing that April's presents would lie unwrapped in the cupboard was tearing me apart.

In late November, I made the decision to go shopping in Aberystwyth to get the last of what I needed. Paul and I could have happily forgotten about the festive season but that wouldn't have been fair on Jazmin and Harley.

For someone who used to be very independent, I now couldn't face being on my own and I literally wouldn't leave the house without someone I trusted by my side. My life had completely changed in the space of a few short weeks. Some of our friends and neighbours had been wonderfully supportive but, as the dust settled, others distanced themselves. On the rare occasions I did venture out, I'd often see people I'd known for years cross the street to avoid me. I suppose they were so scared of saying the wrong thing that they chose to say nothing at all. It was incredibly hurtful.

Paul agreed to come shopping with me. I'd spent so long locked away in my room, only leaving when I absolutely had to, that I had no idea what going to a busy shopping centre would be like.

I immediately felt out of my depth and we were both tearful. Paul was trying his best to hold it together for my sake, but I could tell he was struggling. This would be the first of many Christmases without April and it was so unfair.

Even though it was a weekday, the shops were packed with people. Out of the corner of my eye, I could see people nudging each other and pointing to us. It's astonishing how people can think they are being discreet when they're so blatantly talking about you.

Others didn't attempt to be subtle, approaching us directly as if they'd known us their whole lives. I lost count of the number of people who called my name.

'Mrs Jones!' one woman exclaimed, rushing towards me as we walked along the main street. 'Mrs Jones! You're April's mum!'

She was around my age and I began to wonder if I knew her, but I didn't recognise her face. I gripped Paul's hand tightly but, before I knew it, she launched herself at me and wrapped her arms around me, enveloping me into a hug. I'd been caught completely off guard and I felt trapped. My hands were sweaty and my heart was hammering. Instead of feeling comforted, I felt suffocated, to the point where I was on the verge of a panic attack. Even when I broke free from her, shaking and barely able to breathe, she was undeterred.

'I just wanted you to know I was there,' she said.

'Excuse me?' Paul replied.

'I just wanted to say hello,' she went on, absolutely oblivious to how much she had upset us. 'Just because I hadn't seen you since the night it all happened, when I came down to help look.'

Neither of us could find any words to answer her. She sounded almost proud of herself.

'I was actually speaking to you,' she said to Paul. 'Don't you remember?'

'Sorry,' he replied, shaking his head. 'I don't.'

Soon afterwards, we mumbled our excuses and left. Of course, things are a bit of a blur and it's possible that she did speak to Paul, albeit briefly, but to be ambushed by a stranger when you're already distressed is terrifying. We got home about 4 p.m. that night and I went to bed, wiped out. I knew people would never treat me normally again and it was a horrible thought.

Christmas shopping knocked me for six for a few days, which was a strange feeling. I'd always been a big kid at Christmas. I loved spoiling the children and everyone on Bryn-y-Gog loved my elaborate decorations – lots of lights, tinsel and Christmas teddies that could sing and dance. By mid-November, I'd be itching to get them up and, as April had got older, she'd loved helping out. Her favourite decoration was a dancing penguin with a little bell. When she was in one of her mischievous moods, she'd pull the bell off and giggle until her face was red.

This year, the idea of putting a few baubles on the tree filled me with absolute dread but I knew I had to keep things as normal as possible for Jazmin and Harley, so I asked my friend Ceri to help us. I wasn't prepared to go all out but I wanted the house to look a little bit festive.

Ceri and her husband AJ had a coffee with Paul and me, before he took the dogs for a walk and the rest of us started to put some decorations up outside the house. We were wrestling with an inflatable snowman when, out of nowhere, Dave and Hayley were coming up the path.

'Oh, hi,' I said. 'We weren't expecting you until later.'

'Coral,' Dave replied, skipping the usual pleasantries. 'Is Paul here?'

'No, he's out walking the dogs,' I said. As I noticed the grim expressions on his and Hayley's faces, I felt panic grip me. 'Why?'

'You have to phone him,' Dave said. 'He needs to come home now.'

As soon as I got the call from Coral, I raced home. Thankfully I hadn't gone far and was only a few minutes from the house. I was convinced they'd found April's body and I felt violently sick. Three days before, Dave had come round and we'd talked about the case, perhaps in more detail than we'd ever done before. From this conversation, it was clear that the police believed Bridger had taken April home before killing her and disposing of her body somewhere in the vast countryside surrounding his cottage. I could only hope they were going to put us out of our misery and tell us where our little girl was.

'What's going on?' I said, as I burst through the front door. The colour had drained from Coral's face.

'Hi, Paul,' Dave said. 'Andy John is in Machynlleth. We've just had a call from him. He'd like to meet you at the sanctuary now.'

'Have they found her?' I cried, unable to keep my emotions in check.

'All we know is that there is some new forensic evidence,' replied Dave, in a measured tone. 'We should go.'

But bile was rising in my throat and I rushed upstairs to the bathroom, where I vomited for several minutes, overcome by dread and nerves. I didn't want to go back downstairs, but I knew I had to. On the one hand, I hoped they'd found April, as the nightmare of wondering where she was would be over. We could also have a funeral and begin to grieve properly. But on the other hand it was all so final. Would Andy be able to tell us what Bridger had done to her? I didn't know if I could cope with hearing how he'd made my little girl suffer and I was pretty sure it would kill Coral.

Somehow I found the strength to get into the car and we made the short journey in virtual silence. Andy had already briefed Dave and Hayley about what the forensic teams had found, but they'd agreed he would be the one to tell us, so we could only guess what this news was going to be. We were in the car for only a few minutes, but it seemed like hours.

Andy was already waiting in the sanctuary when we arrived. I instantly felt sorry for him. Every time we met with him, he had to break bad news to us. But he always did his best to be as sensitive as he could towards us and tell us straight, which was what we wanted. For this reason, we didn't hold any grudges. On that day, it felt like an eternity before he spoke.

'OK,' he began. 'I'm afraid we've had some bleak forensic results. When the forensic teams were examining Mark Bridger's house, they found a wood burner. Amongst the ashes, they found some human remains.'

Neither Coral nor I said anything, but Hayley grabbed hold of Coral's hand.

'The remains are only small,' Andy went on. 'There are five pieces in total and they measure about 20mm in diameter. They are from a human skull. We believe them to be April's but we can't prove this yet.'

I expected Coral to be hysterical, but she was remarkably calm as she met Andy's eye.

'So,' she said. 'He's smashed her to bits then?'

Andy bowed his head.

'What you're saying is, he's cut off her head and burned it?' I asked, picking up where Coral had left off.

'I'm afraid it's looking that way,' Andy replied.

'What about the rest of her body?' I said. I was hearing the words that were being said to me, but my mind had not yet caught up.

'We don't yet have any evidence of any other body parts,' Andy said.

Andy stayed for a few more minutes, before leaving us alone with Dave and Hayley, who helped talk us through what we'd just been told. After he'd gone, the shock wore off and we both became very emotional. Coral cried silently for the rest of the meeting. I had tears in my eyes, but I was trying my hardest to be strong for my wife. Even in our worst nightmares, neither of us had predicted a scenario like this. Bridger had snatched our precious daughter, but he hadn't just killed her – he'd completely destroyed her. Imagining the terror our little girl would have felt in her final moments – not to mention what she would have suffered – had already begun to eat us both up inside. All we could hope was that it had been quick and that she'd died before he did the worst of the damage.

'Why haven't they found her teeth?' I said. 'Surely the fire couldn't be hot enough to burn enamel?'

'Children's milk teeth are different,' Dave said. 'They have small holes in them.'

Dave and Hayley told us once again how important it was that we didn't share this news with anyone. Even the search teams were unaware of this development. Although the search for April was still ongoing, Dave told us that if they found anything, it was likely to be just a torso, though even this may have been burned and hidden.

The worst thing of all was that if no more of April's remains were found, we were unlikely to be allowed to have a funeral until after the trial. The bone fragments would form a key part of the prosecution case and couldn't be released until the court case was over. More than anything we wanted justice for April, so we understood how important this was, but it didn't make things any easier, especially as we couldn't even say a proper goodbye.

That night, Coral and I lay in bed holding each other and silently crying. It was a few days before we could bear to have a conversation about what we'd been told. How do you begin to talk about the possibility that someone chopped off your daughter's head and burned it in a log fire? We were nothing more than pawns in Bridger's sick game.

The worst thing was having to keep information from our loved ones. We were carrying a huge burden that we couldn't share, even with some of the people who loved April most, like our parents and siblings. The biggest dilemma of all was what we'd tell Jazmin and Harley, who still seemed to think April was alive and being hidden by her kidnapper. Harley in particular was hopeful they'd be reunited with her soon. He even asked us if she'd be home for Christmas, which was heartbreaking. We didn't want to keep anything from either of them, but we decided to get the holidays out of the way before we had a frank conversation about how their sister had been murdered. If nothing else, they deserved the best Christmas we could possibly give them.

'April, I was so looking forward to watching you grow up,' I wrote in my diary that evening. 'It's not like we have a lot to look forward to. We have no money. My eyes are bad and my prospects are dire. I think I put some of my hope for life in you, but now you leave such a hole in my life. We just don't know what to do, or how to carry on, but we must. We will have to tell Jazz and Harley sometime in January. It will break their hearts and mess them up even more than now, but they need us and your mum and I need each other.

'I love you, April. Dad xxx.'

6

Limbo

We knew there wouldn't be any major developments in the case before Christmas was over, so we had no choice but to wait. Luckily, our FLOs were very supportive and keen to answer any questions we might have. A few weeks before Christmas, they organised a meeting with the Crown Prosecution Service so we could speak about the case.

When we arrived at the meeting, our emotions were on a knife edge. It had been a very mixed morning. The post had arrived early and with it two important letters. The first was from Prince William and his wife Kate. Just a few days earlier it had been announced that they were expecting their first baby, after Kate had been hospitalised with severe morning sickness. Prince William wrote that although he was sure his letter was of no worth, he couldn't bear not to get in touch to say how sorry he was about April. We were overwhelmed that, amongst everything he was dealing with, the future King had found the time to contact us and offer his condolences.

The next letter was not so uplifting. It was from the local council, who advised us that they would shortly be removing all the pink bows on display in the town centre. Coral especially found this insensitive and highly unnecessary. Making the bows had been a coping mechanism for her and had really helped us both see how much support there was for our family in the town. April had barely been gone two months and we still had the trial to get through. We had always understood that the town needed to move on at some point but all our friends and neighbours were still mourning the loss of April. Coral was very tearful and when Dave and Hayley heard how upset she'd become, they were very angry. They immediately arranged a meeting with the councillors to find out how the decision had been made and if it could be reversed.

By mid-morning I was stressed and in desperate need of fresh air. I took a walk up my hill with Autumn and Storm and, when I reached the top, I realised I was crying. I sat down for a few moments and began to speak to April. As well as writing in my diary, I'd taken to doing this on my quiet moments on the hill as it helped me feel close to my little girl.

'We miss and love you so much,' I sobbed. 'I promise I'll look after your mum, Jazz, Harley and all of your teddies.'

Right at that moment, I noticed a faint rainbow had begun to appear over Bryn-y-Gog. I'd made scores, if not hundreds, of trips up this hill but I'd never seen a rainbow before. I strained my eyes and realised its arch was covering the exact spot where we believed April was taken. As it grew brighter, I saw that it had stretched right from Penrath, where I'd spent so many happy moments with April, to Ceinws, where she'd most likely breathed her last. I started to cry again, but my tears were now a mix of sadness and a strange sort of joy. April loved rainbows and she always sang about them in her little improvised songs, using the Welsh word *enfys*.

The rainbow remained as I trudged back down the hill. It seemed to grow more vibrant each time I looked at it. Neither Coral nor I are religious but, while Coral believes in the possible existence of angels, I have always been a little more sceptical. Before April was taken, I was more or less of the opinion that death was final – that all of our thoughts and feelings ceased to exist at the end of our life.

Now it's tempting to think there might be an afterlife. I wouldn't say I was a believer, but I keep an open mind. April was so at one with the countryside and I went to my hill to feel close to her. It would be lovely to think that her spirit lived on, that the rainbow was her way of communicating with me – but I guess I'll never know for sure.

When I got home, there wasn't much time before the meeting, so I quickly showered and changed before Dave and Hayley arrived to take us to the sanctuary. We'd be meeting with Ewan Jenkins of the Crown Prosecution Service as well as Andy. Ewan was a very nice man and answered all of our questions as best he could.

'Do you think Mark Bridger could be convicted, even though we don't have April's body?' I asked.

'Considering the forensic evidence we have, I'm very confident,' he said. 'If he isn't, I'll eat my words.'

'I'll remember you said that,' I replied. We both laughed, but in my case it was more through relief than anything else. Ewan had given us the news we wanted to hear. For a fleeting moment I allowed myself to wonder if maybe, just maybe, the rainbow had been a sign after all. If Mark Bridger was locked up in jail, he couldn't hurt any more children. Could this be April's way of telling us everything was going to be OK? In the end, I decided not to dwell on the unanswered questions and focus on things that seemed more certain – we had a good case and we had to concentrate on getting through the trial.

But I was soon to be brought back down to earth with a crushing blow. I'd noticed my eyesight had worsened over the past few weeks, though I'd largely ignored the changes as I'd been so preoccupied. However, when I went for a routine examination, my optician told me that I'd failed my basic vision test, meaning my eyesight had deteriorated so much I could now be registered legally blind. It's amazing what trauma can do to the human body.

Coral and I also decided to accept an invitation to go to the school's Christmas fair. The school had been so good to Harley, it seemed a shame to miss it and in a way it was uplifting to see the children running around, excited for the festive season. But it was also a stark and crushing reminder of what we'd lost.

'April, I think about you every day,' I wrote that evening. 'I cry most nights. I always look in and say goodnight and send you a kiss but, as Christmas comes, I miss you and I can't bear to see your empty bed.'

By now, hot tears were stinging my eyes, as I carefully formed the words with my pen. As my vision deteriorated, it got harder and harder to write but I couldn't bear to give up.

'I find myself crying and I don't know why,' I continued. 'I'll get through this because I love you and I know you love me. This alone is enough for me. I wish to hear your voice, to see your smile, to kiss you goodnight. But my memory will have to do. I miss you, my beautiful, brown-eyed girl.

'Lots of love, your very sad Dad xxx.'

Coral didn't write down her feelings in the way I did, but there was no mistaking how low she was. Three days before Christmas, she decided to take an afternoon nap. I knew she wanted to be alone, but it tore me apart as I listened to her crying for three whole hours, barely stopping for breath.

It was a horrendous day and the rain had been battering the windows for hours, which mirrored the solemn mood in the house. As Machynlleth is located in a valley, it floods easily and some of the roads were already shut. Even I, with my love of the outdoors, was in no mood to venture outside.

In an attempt to cheer everybody up, I made chips, eggs and bacon for dinner, which I served up to Sue, who'd arrived from Holyhead a few days earlier, Jazmin and Harley. I made my way upstairs and tentatively knocked on the bedroom door.

'Would you like some dinner, love?' I asked Coral.

'I'm not hungry,' came the weak reply.

I didn't expect her to surface for the rest of the evening, so I was surprised when she came downstairs around half an hour later. Her face was blotchy and tear-stained but she was fully clothed.

'I'm going out,' she announced.

'You can't go out in this weather!' I protested.

'I need some petrol for the car,' she said, vacantly, grabbing her keys and closing the door behind her.

'I'm really worried,' I said to Sue. 'She can't drive in that rain. I'm going to call Dave.'

Dave was relaxing at home with his wife, but as soon as I told him what was going on, he jumped in the car and told me he'd be in Machynlleth as soon as he could. I tried to ring Coral a few times, but it kept going to voicemail, which only worried me more.

'Where's Mum?' Harley kept asking, over and over.

'I don't know, Harley,' I replied, trying to sound calm. 'She'll be back soon, don't worry.'

I hoped that I sounded convincing.

Coral recalls:

As I listened to the sound of the rain on our roof on that horrible Saturday afternoon, the pain inside me was so great I thought it might kill me there and then. April would have been so excited about Christmas she'd hardly be sleeping. Instead, there was a huge void in all of our lives and nothing would ever be the same again.

I sobbed for hours but eventually my grief turned to anger. I thought about Bridger in his prison cell. Was he thinking about what he'd done to my little girl? Was he proud of smashing her to pieces and throwing her remains in a fire, like she was a piece of rubbish? He wasn't suffering like I was. We couldn't even have a funeral for our baby because he wouldn't tell us what he'd done with her. There wasn't a shred of humanity in his body.

I imagined him being tortured by other inmates every day for the rest of his life before dying a slow, painful death, but that brought me no real comfort. All I needed was a hug from my little girl and I'd never get one again. I wanted to close my curtains and hide under the covers and never come out, but at the same time I wanted to bang the walls and scream with rage.

After several hours, I realised I couldn't take any more. I had to get out of the house, with all its painful reminders of the Christmases we'd shared with April. I know I should have told Paul where I was going, but I didn't even know myself.

With the wind howling around me, I clambered into the car and turned the key in the ignition. The thirty-second walk from the house had left me soaked through, but I could barely even feel the rain on my skin. I flicked on the windscreen wipers but it was getting heavier by the minute. I only managed to drive a few miles along one of the back roads near Machynlleth before I had to pull over. Pulling on the handbrake, I collapsed on the steering wheel and started to cry again.

I wasn't aware of how quickly the road was flooding, or how long I'd been gone. Of course I later felt terrible for the worry I'd caused my family, but when your grief is so intense it's hard to focus on anything but your own agony.

I almost jumped out of my skin when I heard a knock on the window and I was surprised to see Dave standing outside, drenched. I didn't know that Paul had been so worried he'd called him and Dave had set out to find me. The road was now badly flooded and he couldn't get his car through, so he'd hitched a lift with a farmer who'd been passing in a 4×4. It was a mark of how dedicated our FLOs were that they were willing to be on 24-hour call, even at Christmas time.

I opened the door and he climbed into the passenger side without saying anything.

'He's had three meals today,' I wept. 'He's warm.'

Dave didn't have to ask who I was referring to.

'I know, Coral,' he said. 'It's totally shit.'

Dave phoned home to say I was safe. We chatted for a while and, when the rain had eased off, we drove back to the police station, where we met Paul. He looked relieved and gave me a hug, but I was still numb. It was going to be a difficult few days.

By Christmas Eve, we were both feeling sick with stress, wondering how we'd get through the next day. In need of some thinking time, I took the dogs for a walk around the outskirts of Machynlleth. Walking past the golf course, I was caught off guard when I saw a poster with April's face on it. Before I knew it, I had sunk to my knees, sobbing. I stayed there for a long time, as Autumn and Storm tried to comfort me.

The next morning, Harley awoke, full of beans at 6.30 a.m. Coral and I couldn't face the thought of getting up, so we told a little white lie and said it was only 4.30 a.m. so we could have a little extra time in bed. We eventually got up at 7.30 a.m. and trudged downstairs to open our presents.

Harley was delighted with his television and Xbox games. Jazmin was a little quieter, but thanked us for the clothes and make-up we'd bought her. I was on the verge of tears and I could tell Coral wasn't doing much better. No one mentioned April's name, but we didn't need to. She was all we could think about.

Then, Jazmin gave us a photo album she'd put together. It had lots of family pictures, including some of April. It was a lovely gift, but I couldn't look at Coral because I knew I'd burst into tears if I caught her eye.

Coral tried her best to do the traditional turkey dinner with all the trimmings. It was delicious, but none of us had much of an appetite. We were relieved when Tracey popped in for a few hours. It was kind of her to think of us, as she has a family of her own and most mums are too busy on Christmas Day to spare any time for anyone else. She really lightened the mood and we even found ourselves laughing a little. But when she left, we all felt flat. We tried to watch some Christmas films, but it just didn't feel right. While everyone went to bed, I reached for my diary.

'April, today is a day for young boys and girls,' I wrote. 'But, while we go on without you, it doesn't mean we'll ever forget. I know I'll never accept it. I don't think I'll ever stop hoping or loving you. I keep going for Mum, Jazz and Harley and I'll look after your darling dogs, Autumn and Storm.'

The next few days were even worse. On Boxing Day, the house was like a morgue. Coral was very emotional at how quiet it was without April and things only got worse when she noticed a comment on Facebook from someone who claimed to have seen April on the night she disappeared. We called Dave, who made inquiries and quickly established that this person had seen April playing on another evening and wasn't required as a witness. Still, it seemed irresponsible and insensitive that someone could post information like this on Facebook instead of going to the police.

Then, the day before New Year's Eve, Coral was tidying up when she suddenly became very distressed and threw two pot plants out of the door, shaking and sobbing violently. It was so unlike her to behave in this way that I was really alarmed and eventually had to phone one of her friends to help calm her down. After a bit of coaxing, we discovered she'd found April's birth tag from hospital. It was hardly surprising she was so upset. Our daughter had fought so hard to come into this world, only to be taken from it so senselessly. But what worried me most was that I'd never found it so hard to reach Coral before. We'd always been on the same wavelength and, even since April had gone, we tried our hardest not to fall down at the same time so we could pick each other up. But the festive season was testing us like never before and we found ourselves snapping at each other a few times, unable to deal with the pressure. For the first time, I began to understand how much we'd have to work on our relationship as well as keeping strong for the children and dealing with our own grief. Every day seemed like more of a struggle than the last.

To make matters worse, we had our first proper court visit looming over us – the day we'd finally see our daughter's suspected killer in the flesh for the first time since he'd taken her. This was only a preliminary appearance and unlikely to last any more than a day, but the thought of coming face to face with Bridger was making me very anxious. Coral was still determined she wanted to face him. Considering how vulnerable she'd been of late, I was even more convinced I had to put my misgivings to one side and accompany her.

Before the hearing, the police arranged for us to meet the prosecution barrister, Elwen Evans, at a local hotel. Both Coral and I were nervous, as there were to be several people from the Crown Prosecution Service and the police, too, and we hoped we wouldn't feel suffocated or swamped with information. To add to this, the meeting was scheduled for 9 January, the 100th day since April had gone missing and we were both feeling very low.

Elwen was a formidable woman and an even more formidable lawyer. One of the most respected and feared QCs in Wales, she struck fear into the hearts of anyone who crossed her in the courtroom. We were immediately glad to have her on our side. She was calm, spoke elegantly, and straight away made us feel at ease in her company.

'The indications are that Mark Bridger will plead not guilty,' she told us. 'He's very sure of himself, but this is good because he'll talk quite a lot.'

'What do you mean?' I asked.

'In doing this, he'll give us opportunities to take his case apart,' Elwen explained.

'I hope he takes the stand because I would like to see you take him apart,' I said.

'I would dearly love to,' she replied.

Elwen also thanked us for not speaking to the press about the court case. She explained that, if we'd chosen to do so, this could allow Bridger's lawyer to claim he hadn't been given a fair trial. If someone had been selected to be on the jury after reading an emotional interview with us about April, they may have struggled to be impartial when presented with the evidence.

'We're very grateful you've maintained a dignified silence,' she told us.

'We just don't want to take anything away from April,' Coral said. 'We need to get justice for her.'

Andy was also there and he explained that some new evidence

against Mark Bridger had come to light. The police had recovered his computer and had found pornographic images of children. This suggested his crimes may have been premeditated, although they didn't think April was necessarily the intended victim. Naturally this made Coral and me sick to our stomachs, but we'd got to the stage where nothing surprised us and were pleased that the case against Bridger seemed as strong as it did.

I felt unusually positive when I picked up my diary that night.

'April, I feel reassured now I've met all these amazing people,' I wrote. 'I think we're in good hands with people who take pride in their jobs and truly want the best for you.

'I love you, Dad xxx.'

7

Facing the Monster

Bridger's court appearance posed some questions for Coral and me. The first was what to tell Jazmin and Harley. Coral was very stressed, as one of the local papers had published a piece about the hearing, and she was scared one of them would see it by mistake, or that someone would mention it in passing. We asked Dave and Hayley for their advice but they told us it might be better to wait until we came back from court to speak to our children properly about what had happened. It would be a very emotional conversation and, right now, we needed to save our strength to face the monster who took our baby from us.

The second was, quite obviously, how we would feel when we saw Bridger in the flesh. In my darkest moments, I was certain I wouldn't be able to restrain myself – that I'd want to climb over the seats, push past the security guards and do to him what he did to my little girl. But, more than anything, I was worried about Coral. I wasn't sure how she'd react, sitting so close to the man who killed her baby girl, as much as she said she wanted to face him.

At one point the previous week, it had looked like Bridger would not have to appear in court. Instead, he wanted to make his plea via video link. However, the judge, Mr Justice John Griffith-Williams, insisted he appear in person. Coral and I were divided on this. I had no real desire to see Bridger – in fact, I was scared of how I'd react if I did – but she was adamant it was something we had to do.

Our FLOs had arranged for us to stay on the outskirts of Mold the night before the hearing, as they didn't want us to go to court in the morning after a long car journey. Before they picked us up, I took a long walk with the dogs, as I needed time to think. As usual, I climbed my favourite hill and tied a pink ribbon to the fence as I spoke to April. I couldn't think of much to say, so I simply told her we loved and missed her.

When I got back to the house, Dave was already there. I got myself washed and changed and said goodbye to Jazmin and Harley before stopping to take one last look in April's bedroom. It never seemed to get any easier, seeing her teddies spread out on the bed without her.

'We're doing this for you, honey,' I whispered, before closing the door.

Dave drove us to the sanctuary, where we'd arranged to meet Hayley. There was a bit of a panic when she called to say she was having trouble getting over the mountain road that links

Machynlleth to nearby Llanidloes. It had been snowing heavily and the driving conditions were poor, with lots of vehicles getting stuck. Thankfully, she managed to get on the road again and arrived shortly afterwards.

My Uncle Trevor and his wife Vicky had agreed to meet us at our hotel and it was nice to relax with them for a few hours and have some beers. We discussed how nervous we were about seeing Bridger. But Uncle Trevor also shares my love of tinkering with motorbikes and we spoke about the bikes he was doing up. The change of subject certainly helped ease my mind and, when they left just before midnight, I felt slightly more relaxed.

Coral went to bed and I got out my diary and started to write. Putting my thoughts down on paper had become almost compulsive.

'Coral says she's ready for tomorrow,' I wrote. 'I hope she'll be OK, seeing the man who killed her baby girl. It will be devastating for me, but what it will be like for a mother I can't imagine. She's my biggest worry, but I'm also worried for Harley and Jazz at home. I hope they're OK. The press will be out in force tomorrow. I don't know how we will handle it.

'I love you April. Dad xxx.'

It soon became obvious we'd never get a good night's sleep. I dozed off for a bit but my mind was too busy to rest. After hours of tossing and turning, we admitted defeat at 5.30 a.m. and huddled together on the bed watching television for a few hours before we had to get up. We then showered and put on the pink shirts we'd selected for the day, both pinning pink bows to them. This was our way of feeling like April was with us.

Dave and Hayley picked us up just before 9 a.m. and drove us to the court. They'd warned us that there would be lots of press in attendance and they weren't wrong. Outside the court steps, there were reporters, photographers and television crews, all waiting for our arrival. We'd already agreed that we would use the main entrance to the court to allow them one photo opportunity before the hearing started. On Dave and Hayley's advice, we reasoned that once they'd got the picture they needed, they'd be more likely to leave us alone for the rest of the day.

We were led into a small box room, with a little television. There was also tea and coffee. We were told that this would be our private area for the duration of the case, as we weren't allowed to mix with the witnesses in the larger holding room. It might have been small, but it was nice to know we had our own space.

We had a cup of tea with Dave and Hayley while we waited for Bridger to arrive but, as the minutes ticked by, it became obvious the van carrying him from prison was late. When we were eventually called through to the main courtroom half an hour later, I instinctively grabbed Coral's hand.

'Here goes,' I said.

Coral recalls:
I'd been determined that Paul and I should go to court to see Bridger in the flesh. He had to face us and face what he'd done to us. I wanted him to see the agony in our faces, to look at us in the eye and see how he'd ripped us apart.

In the days leading up to the hearing, I'd had so many lovely messages from friends and strangers alike, wishing us well. There were literally hundreds and I'd never have had time to read them all, but I was grateful to everyone who'd taken the time to write to us or message us on Facebook.

I couldn't speak publicly about the case, as neither Paul nor I dared do anything that might jeopardise Bridger's right to a fair trial. It was beyond ridiculous that we were so keen to protect the rights of the man who'd butchered our child but the idea of him being acquitted on a technicality was more than we could stand. We had to get justice for April, if it was the last thing we did.

It felt like the longest half an hour of my life, waiting for the prison van to arrive, but when it did I wasn't sure how to feel. Walking into the court, I felt my throat tighten at the sight of the crowds of people but I had to stay strong.

I was glad we didn't have to walk through the packed room with hundreds of eyes boring into us, as we made our way up the aisle. Instead, we were led straight from our little room to the front row, where Dave sat on Paul's side and Hayley on mine.

Bridger was brought out almost straight away and led into the glass-screened dock, no more than ten feet from us, with guards on either side of him. I grabbed Paul's hand and my cheeks burned as hatred tore through me. Bridger was no different to what we'd remembered, apart from the fact his hair had grown a little. He looked scruffy in his blue jumper and jeans and he had the beginnings of a beard. How could a man who appeared so insignificant be capable of such evil?

Both Paul and I fixed our eyes on him but he looked down to his right, refusing to meet our gaze. As I stared at him, I imagined my eyes were lasers, slowly burning his skin. I was vaguely aware of the legal argument going on around me but the voices of lawyers drifted into the background.

This man had destroyed our lives for a few sick minutes of pleasure, to fulfil a fantasy so disgusting I couldn't bear to think of it. I wanted him to know how I felt as I lay in my bed for days on end, crying so hard I was in genuine, physical pain. I wanted him to know how we felt when we opened April's bedroom door and saw her empty bed; how we felt on Christmas morning, knowing her presents were lying unwrapped in a cupboard. I wanted him to know how we felt thinking of the rest of our lives stretching out in front of us without April – a huge, gaping void that would only get wider as the years went on.

But, as he pretended to wipe a tear from his eye, I almost laughed. He didn't care about us. His only concern was for himself and the realisation that his lies that had finally caught up with him.

I think I might have been crying myself – I have a hazy memory of dabbing my eyes with a tissue but I was so caught up in my thoughts that I couldn't say for sure.

I started to think about what it would be like if I had a nail gun, if someone in the row behind me just happened to pass me one. He was so close to me that if everyone turned their backs for a moment maybe, just maybe, I'd be able to get to him. My eyes still on him, I imagined piercing his skin over and over, nail after nail after nail, hearing his screams as he begged me to stop. But even then he wouldn't be suffering half as much as we were.

I squeezed Coral's hand as tightly as I could the whole way through the hearing. When Bridger was brought into the dock, my nerves almost evaporated and a strange sense of calm came over me. He looked pathetic. We had the power now – he couldn't scare us. The case against him was mounting and we hoped that soon he'd be rotting behind bars for the rest of his life.

In the first part of the hearing, Bridger's barrister, Brendan Kelly QC, asked Mr Justice Griffith-Williams if the trial could be moved away from mid-Wales. He argued that there was too much 'ill feeling' towards Bridger here and that this would affect his right to a fair trial. Thankfully the judge declined this request, telling him that Mold had specifically been selected to make it as easy as possible for Coral and me to attend. He added that he felt there were sufficient safeguards within the jury system to ensure that Bridger would receive as impartial a hearing as possible.

We weren't surprised when Bridger pleaded not guilty to murdering and kidnapping April. He also denied perverting the course of justice by unlawfully disposing of, destroying or concealing her body. This was the only time he spoke, in a hushed tone, barely more than a whisper.

Brendan Kelly told the court that, although his client didn't accept that he murdered April, he believed he may have killed her by accident. This was not news to us, as Andy had already told us about his claims that he'd run her over in his car, but we were still dumbstruck that anyone could think this was remotely believable – especially now we had so much forensic evidence. I was more convinced than ever that we had a strong case.

Thankfully Brendan Kelly didn't attempt to get Bridger out on bail – he'd be a dead man if he walked down any street in Britain. The trial date was set for 25 February and the hearing was over almost as soon as it had begun.

We thanked our legal team before making a quick exit. We knew the media were congregating outside and we'd already begun to feel light-headed, through a combination of adrenaline and lack of sleep. We stopped for a quick lunch on the way home with Dave and Hayley and arrived back in Machynlleth just in time for Harley coming home from school.

Coral was completely drained and went straight to bed, while I took the dogs for a walk. We'd made it through the day, but the worst was still to come. We'd been told to expect the trial to last around a month and the prospect of having to see Bridger's face day after day was a horrible thought. What's worse, we still had to tell Harley and Jazmin the truth. We knew we couldn't put it off forever, but it would probably be the most difficult conversation we'd ever have.

That night, as I reached for my diary, my thoughts came tumbling out onto the page.

'Today, Mark Bridger pleaded not guilty,' I wrote. 'I think he's heartless and cruel. It seems like he's getting some pleasure in knowing that we're suffering. We've been through so much and we feel so tired and low but I trust Elwen, the Crown Prosecution Service and the police. Soon we will win a small victory for us but a huge victory for society.

'April, all of this is for you. If they knew you, they would love you but even those who didn't do. You have touched a whole nation and indeed the world. Those brown eyes just say it all. Some days, words can't say what I feel, so with tears of love I'll sign off.

'Your ever loving Dad xxx.'

8

Preparing for the Trial

The day after we came home from Mold, we decided to tell Jazmin and Harley that April wouldn't be coming home. Now Bridger had pled not guilty, there would be lots of speculation about the trial and we didn't want to keep anything from them. It was unthinkable that they would hear it from anyone else. We decided that Coral would break the news to them, leaving out some of the most distressing details.

I couldn't even bear to be in the room when Coral told Harley, so I sat downstairs and tried my hardest to block out the sounds of my son's screams.

Coral recalls:
Harley came home from school and had his dinner. He smiled and chatted as usual, with no idea what we were about to tell him. By this point, Jazz had an inkling that things weren't

looking good but Harley still seemed to think his sister was coming home.

'Harley,' I said, taking a deep breath. 'Can you come upstairs for a second?'

He nodded and I took him into his bedroom. I was emotionally drained from the previous day, but it didn't stop my stomach from somersaulting. Inside, I was cursing Bridger. No mother should ever have to tell her ten-year-old son that his sister had been killed.

It made things even worse that two of Bridger's children – we'll call them Josh and Katie – were Harley's best friends. He knew that we'd gone to court and that their dad had been there, accused of taking April, but he didn't know the awful truth of what he'd done with her.

'What's wrong, Mum?' he asked. 'Are you OK?'

'Harley,' I began. 'Do you know why we were at court yesterday?'

He looked confused. 'I think so,' he replied.

'I've got something to tell you and it isn't going to be easy,' I said. 'April won't be coming home. She's been murdered.'

Harley's face turned white and he let out a scream, but not just any scream. I recognised it straight away. It was the same bloodcurdling, piercing scream he'd let out on the night April had been taken.

I didn't know what to do so I just grabbed him and held him to me. There were no more words.

It took a long time for him to calm down. He was crying and stamping his feet so loudly that Paul could hear him downstairs. I would have given anything to take his pain away.

Harley and April had been two peas in a pod, partners in crime. Now, he would grow older while April would be frozen in time, nothing more than a memory, aged five-and-a-half forever. Never again would they get to slide down the stairs in their sleeping bags or practise their wrestling moves. They'd never go to the pub together when they were older or get to know each other's children.

When he'd calmed down, we went back downstairs, where the news was playing in the background. By coincidence, an item about April popped up. I decided to let Harley watch it, as they weren't allowed to report on the forensic evidence. I didn't want him to think we were keeping anything from him. He was fairly quiet and didn't ask any questions.

Later that night, I told Jazz. She had tears in her eyes but she was a lot more subdued than Harley. She's never been one to wear her heart on her sleeve and I think she'd known for a long time what was coming, but I knew her mind was working overtime.

The next day, Dave and Hayley had a more in-depth chat with her. They wanted to make sure she understood the implications of what she'd been told. As she was a little older, they knew she was more likely to pick up on rumours about the case. Again, she was fairly quiet, but Dave and Hayley told her that, if she ever had any questions, she could ask them and they would try their best to answer them. Neither Paul nor I expected her to take their offer so seriously.

She spent a few hours upstairs on her own and soon came up with lots of things she wanted to ask about the case. We were astounded – the questions showed a level of understanding we'd never have expected from a teenager, especially considering the emotional turmoil she was facing when she thought of them. Dave and Hayley were similarly impressed and remarked that most adults in her position wouldn't have been able to think about the investigation so rationally and in such detail. It was obvious that, like the rest of us, Jazz just craved answers about what had happened to her beloved sister.

She asked:

How did the police know Mark Bridger was responsible?
How much blood was there?
How long will it take to find out if it is April?
What is most likely to have happened?
What happened to April's clothes?
Would all of April's remains have been burnt?

Dave and Hayley tried to give detailed answers to as many of the questions as they could. They explained that the police knew Bridger had taken April because a witness had seen her get into his vehicle. They made the decision to tell Jazmin about some of the forensic evidence, as they thought it was important she understood how they had come to the conclusion that April was dead. Dave told her they'd found evidence of a significant puddle of blood on the floor of Bridger's cottage, plus some smaller spots in other parts of the house. He said that the blood had already been DNA tested and the results showed it belonged to April. They explained there were still some questions they couldn't answer – they told Jazz that Bridger had probably killed April with a blow to the head, but they might never know for sure. They also told her they didn't know where all of her remains were, or what had happened to her clothes. Jazz seemed to take all of this on board and Paul and I could only hope the conversation went some way towards helping her come to terms with everything.

As the trial edged closer, Coral and I began counselling. We were a bit sceptical at first – how could speaking to a stranger ease the agony of losing our little girl? But, as time went on, we started to see the benefit of these sessions. The counsellors didn't take away our pain, but they did help us learn how to manage it.

I found myself opening up about the dark thoughts I was having. Given the limited information we had on how Bridger had killed our daughter, we had both become almost delirious wondering what had happened to her. Sometimes I'd find myself lying in April's bed, cuddling her teddies and crying for hours on end as thousands of nightmare scenarios rushed through my head.

'I was listening to the school kids playing in the primary school today,' I wrote in my diary, a few days after we'd broken the news to Jazmin and Harley. Coral and I were both feeling very emotional as, a few days afterwards, it had been Harley's eleventh birthday, and we'd had to put a brave face on. 'You and your friends would be there, April. The school is only 250 metres away. I feel very down, very sorry for myself and for you. Can't stop thinking of you. Did you suffer? Were you scared? How did he kill you? I have pulled myself apart thinking about it on my own.

'April, I miss you so much. I think of you and send you my love every day. I wish you were here in my arms.

'Love you, Dad xxx.'

*

There were also lots of arrangements to be made for the trial. We were likely to be away from home for a month and we knew it wouldn't be practical to travel to and from Mold every day. Dave and Hayley managed to find a cottage on the outskirts of the town, in which we could stay during the week, as we'd already planned to spend our weekends at home in Machynlleth. It was perfect, as it gave us the privacy we needed and the press were unlikely to discover where we were.

This meant we'd need to sort out childcare while we were away. Coral and I spent hours drafting a rota of family and friends to look after Jazmin and Harley. We knew this would be hard for all of us; our children are barely out of our sight under normal circumstances. However, we knew we had to do this for April and we were extremely grateful to everyone who volunteered to help out.

Coral and I were worried about Harley. As is to be expected, he started playing up at school a little, though his temper tantrums were few and far between and he seemed to bounce back quickly from them. In truth, we were a little surprised he wasn't misbehaving more. He too was having counselling but appeared to be holding back. We worried that he was scared to grieve for April because he knew how upset we were and this made us feel terribly guilty. But we eventually came to the conclusion that Harley needed to learn to accept things in his own time and it wouldn't serve any purpose to rush him. We just needed to support him as much as we could when he did get upset. I was almost relieved when he climbed into bed with me one evening and began to cry.

'I miss April, Dad,' he said.

'I know,' I replied. 'We all do.'

'I miss seeing her in school,' he went on. 'I'd always see her on Fridays when we had assembly and I wish she was still there.'

I put my arms around him and let him cry for a few minutes before he decided to go back to his own room.

We decided to allow Harley to continue his friendships with Josh and Katie. We can't deny that it was difficult – they were the children of the man who had taken our daughter from us – and it was hard not to have reservations about allowing them to play with Harley as if nothing had happened. But, in the end, we had to take comfort from our son's childlike innocence and acceptance. In his eyes, Josh and Katie were no different to how they'd always been. How could these children be held responsible for the actions of an evil man? To us, Harley's attitude was an inspiration and showed maturity far beyond his eleven years.

Now it's much easier for us to accept his relationships with Josh and Katie. We have nothing against them. In fact, we actually have a degree of sympathy for them. As they grow older, they are going to learn more and more about what their father did to our beloved daughter, and no one can deny that will have a huge effect on them. They may also be subject to bullying and discrimination based on their relationship to someone whose actions they had no control over. For this reason, we've decided not to use their real names in this book and we both hope they continue to have the anonymity they deserve, as they grow older.

During this time we had several meetings with Andy at the sanctuary. As ever, he was patient and willing to answer questions. We'd been told there was a possibility that we might be called as witnesses and neither of us were keen to take the stand, as we knew how fragile we were, but there was no question that we would have done it had it meant getting justice for April. Thankfully, at the end of January, we were given the good news that we weren't required, meaning we could concentrate on supporting each other through the trial.

At the same time, we were told April's death meant we were eligible for £11,000 under the Criminal Injuries Compensation Scheme: £5,500 each for Coral and me. It felt like a slap in the face. How could anyone put a price on our daughter's head? It made us both sick, especially when the news is filled with reports of prisoners claiming much larger sums when they have allegedly been attacked or mistreated in jail. Our instinct was to refuse the money but Dave and Hayley talked us round. As neither of us was fit to work, they reminded us that we had to think of the future, and of Jazmin and Harley and, reluctantly, we decided to accept it.

A few weeks before the trial, we were called to the sanctuary again to meet Andy. There had been quite a few developments in the prosecution case. Now, as many as eighteen bone fragments had been recovered from Mount Pleasant. All apart from one were burnt and recovered from the fire. The remaining piece was unburnt and had been found in a plughole in the bathroom. Some of the burnt fragments had been sent off to Professor Christina Cattaneo, one of the world's leading forensic pathologists and anthropologists, who was based in Milan. The pieces of bone were not large enough to perform DNA tests on, but Andy said he hoped Professor Cattaneo would be able to confirm the gender and age of the person they belonged to.

We were also told we'd have to view some of the pornographic images found on Bridger's computer, many of which involved young children, before we went to court. Andy thought this would be best, as we would likely be very shocked and upset when we saw them.

It was a difficult day. A few hours later, I came home from a walk with the dogs to find Coral and Jazmin slumped on the floor, hugging and crying. They'd found one of April's scrapbooks in which she'd spelled her name and drawn around her left hand. The three of us cried together for a long time that night.

The week before the trial was scheduled to begin, Dave and Hayley took us to the police station in Aberystwyth to go over the details of the case. Andy arrived shortly afterwards and went through the list of witnesses with us over a coffee. He explained that Professor Cattanco had examined the bone fragments and, in her opinion, they belonged to a human juvenile. We were buoyed by this development, as we knew it would be very good for our case. We were also given a tour of the operations room and the chance to meet some of the staff who had worked on the case, which was very humbling.

The next day, we met Andy at the sanctuary with Dave and Hayley and he explained some of the things we might hear Bridger say when he gave evidence in court. His account of what happened was becoming more and more inconsistent. One minute he claimed he'd run April over, the next that he'd accidentally suffocated her. It was a mystery to us what he'd actually say at the trial; I'm not convinced he was sure of this, either. Andy said Bridger was apparently feeling very sorry for himself, telling anyone who would listen that everyone in Machynlleth was out to get him and that he couldn't sleep at night because, in his words, ghosts were calling him. It was so ridiculous we almost laughed.

We were then shown some of the CCTV evidence, which would form part of the case against Bridger in court. The first images were of April, as she skipped in and out of the changing rooms at the leisure centre before her swimming lesson on the day she was taken. This was extremely difficult. April was so energetic and full of life – it was hard to believe she was just hours from death. If only we could have reached into the camera and pulled her to safety as we sat and watched, lumps forming in our throats. But what really brought tears to my eyes was footage of her trying to open a door in the leisure centre. She was so small she couldn't quite manage it. It just reminded me that she wouldn't have stood a chance against a grown man.

Then we were shown pictures of Bridger's car as it sped past the petrol station on the edge of Machynlleth and along the road towards Ceinws. This was heart wrenching – we couldn't see April but we knew she was inside the car. We almost crumbled, knowing the horrors she was about to face.

The final piece of footage was from the morning after April was taken. It showed Bridger walking his dog just a few yards from his house. He looked so calm, like he didn't have a care in the world. In the background, we could see the smoke rising from his chimney. It made me sick to my stomach.

After the CCTV evidence, we were given pictures of the cottage to look at. Although Bridger had done a major clean-up operation, there were arrows pointing to where the blood had been: the hallway, the toilet seat, the living room floor and on the walls. Bridger also had around twenty hunting knives, an axe, a hammer and some saws. One of the knives had been found in the fire. Coral was very distressed and it was all I could do not to break down, too.

It was only when I took out my diary that evening that I allowed myself to cry the tears that had been threatening all day.

'I don't know what my girl suffered,' I wrote. 'I don't think we'll ever really know, but it must have been awful and my heart breaks knowing she suffered at the hands of such an awful man. I just hope it was quick. I know she would have been scared and would have wanted Coral and me.

'I love you, April. I'm so sorry this happened. You're so beautiful and full of life and into everything – a joy to be with.

'I love you xxx.'

A few days later, Dave picked us up to take us to court. Jazmin and Harley were understandably emotional at the prospect of being separated from us, and it was difficult to say goodbye to them. I had tears in my eyes as I hugged Harley goodbye, but I tried hard not to let him see how upset I was. My mum was there to look after the children but neither of us was able to speak as we left. She just wrapped me into a huge hug and we left it at that.

Coral's friend Melere had agreed to come to court with us for part of the trial but she'd had to sign a confidentiality agreement to make sure she didn't tell anyone about any of the forensic evidence. I went with Dave, while Coral and Melere went in Melere's car.

Dave tried to keep the conversation light on the way to Mold, but I was obviously fairly distracted. We were shown to our accommodation, before Melere drove us to the local pub for a bar meal, as none of us could be bothered to cook. We explained what we could to her about the trial, as we knew what she was going to hear would be shocking and we didn't want her getting too upset.

That night, Coral dozed off but I couldn't sleep a wink. I slipped downstairs and watched television for a few hours, before going for a three-mile run. When Coral and Melere got up a few hours later, we were all feeling sick with nerves.

Dave and Hayley picked us up at 10 a.m. as the trial was due to begin at 11 a.m. We dropped Melere off and then Coral and I got out of the car so we could walk to the court steps together for the benefit of the press, who were gathered there. They had been in discussions with the police and had agreed to leave us alone if they were allowed one shot of us walking into the court building. Dave and Hayley hung back a little so they could get Coral and me on our own. Over the next few months, we'd walk past the scrum of photographers many times as we walked into the court, but the blinding light of the flashbulbs never got any less daunting.

We were then taken to our holding room, where we were told the case would be delayed for another hour due to legal argument. The court volunteers made tea and chatted to us. They were very nice people but our minds were on other things. We just wanted to get this over with.

Around 12.30 p.m., we were told Elwen wanted to speak to us, so she was brought to us.

'I'm afraid the trial is likely to be delayed,' she said. I assumed she meant a delay of a few hours, a few days at the most.

'What do you mean?' I asked.

'Mark Bridger is now claiming diminished responsibility,' she explained. 'He wants to argue that he was not of sound mind when he killed April. This means a psychiatric report will have to be carried out, which will take around four weeks.'

'Four weeks!' I echoed. Bridger had killed our little girl, but it felt like he was holding all the cards. Why did he always have the upper hand?

'Then we'll want to get our own psychiatric report done,' Elwen continued. 'So that will take us to Monday, April 29th.'

We knew not to blame Elwen, but Coral and I were both very angry. We'd spent weeks making plans for this trial and we'd psyched ourselves up to face Bridger and hear his lies first-hand. Now the agony would be prolonged, as he tried everything he could to wriggle out of the mess he'd created for himself.

We were taken into court, where the situation was explained for the benefit of the press, although they weren't allowed to report on the reasons for the delay as this could affect Bridger's right to a fair trial. Of course, in our more logical moments, we appreciated how important this was. It would be galling if he got off on a technicality or if he was freed on appeal. However, it was hard not to feel that everything was being done for his benefit and that our rights – not to mention April's – had been momentarily forgotten.

Once again, we were sat just a few feet from him but he avoided making eye-contact with us, his gaze fixed firmly on the ground. He was such a coward he couldn't even look at us. I felt far less calm this time, but I knew it wasn't worth getting emotional or showing him how much he'd got to us. He was so sick he'd probably have enjoyed that.

After the hearing, we returned to our accommodation and

packed our bags. It was only then I realised how exhausted I was. The adrenaline had kept me up all night and now I was beginning to crash. I felt flat and empty when we returned home.

'Coral is very frustrated,' I wrote in my diary that night. I could barely keep my eyes open but I had to vent my emotions. 'It's taken a bit of effort for her to get this far and now we have another eight weeks to get through.

'I'm very tired and I'm shaking with anger and frustration, too. It took a lot for us to get to where we are and we were hoping to relax when everything came out in court, as we can't speak about what we know and we desperately want Mark Bridger to go down forever. The strain on Coral and me is so much, it's like we're not in control. He is still calling the shots.

'I love you, April. Dad xxx.'

The next eight weeks passed in a bit of a blur, as once again we found ourselves in limbo. I started to dream about April more and more vividly each night. One night, I dreamed we were down by the river, throwing stones, as we often did. When each stone hit the water with a splash, April would giggle and beg me to throw another one in. I'd just picked up the biggest stone I could find when suddenly I woke up. Startled, I sat up in bed and it took me a few minutes to realise I'd been in a deep sleep. Then reality hit me like a sledgehammer, as it always does. April was gone and we'd never throw stones in the river together again. I spent the rest of the night crying into my pillow, praying I wouldn't wake Coral. By the time morning came, my eyes were raw.

The delay in the start of the trial meant we had to get on with life as best we could. On the rare occasions we managed to have a fairly normal day, we'd be gripped by guilt that we weren't constantly thinking of April. One day I went to visit some friends in Aberystwyth for coffee, and I actually found myself laughing, as we joked around, barely mentioning the court case. I knew I needed these days in order to stay sane, but it didn't make me feel any better about enjoying them.

'It's days like this I get this guilty dread,' I wrote that evening. 'It's a sad feeling. I've had a normal day but I feel like I'm letting April down by not crying and thinking of her every minute of the day. She is always in my heart, never far from my thoughts.'

To top it all off, those eight weeks brought two important milestones, the first of which was our first wedding anniversary on 13 March. We'd assumed we'd be too caught up in the trial to mark it but now we were at home and we had to face it.

In the end, we didn't do much, as neither of us had any inclination to celebrate. Coral had a bad headache early in the day but was feeling a little better in the evening, so I encouraged her to go to bingo with Jazmin and some friends while I went for a long walk with the dogs. I spent a lot of time thinking about how much had changed in the year since we'd got married and how excited April had been that her mum and dad had finally become husband and wife. None of us could have predicted the awful turn things would take.

The second event was even harder – April's sixth birthday, which would have taken place on 4 April. Unlike our wedding anniversary, we couldn't sit at home and pretend it wasn't happening. This was April's day and we had to mark it.

It was Coral's idea to release pink balloons from the grass outside our house to see how far they would travel. Each of the balloons had a tag on which you could write a message to the person who happened to find it. April would have loved this idea and would have been desperate to see how far her balloon would go.

It was a beautiful spring day, with barely a cloud in the sky. Coral and I spent the whole day blowing up the balloons with the help of friends and family. We'd also made and iced cakes for anyone who wanted to come back to the house afterwards.

The balloons were released around 6.30 p.m. that evening and it was a spectacular sight. In the end, around 750 people had decided to take part, including almost all of the pupils from April's school. Coral was quite tearful, but as I squeezed her hand I hoped there were some happy tears as well as sad ones. I couldn't help but think how April would have squealed with joy had she seen the balloons sailing high above Bryn-y-Gog. The balloons were found in all corners of the UK and one even travelled as far as Germany, where it made the local news. As always, our beautiful daughter was stealing hearts all over the world.

Unsurprisingly there was lots of press interest and the balloons floating off into the sky made for a great photo opportunity. We were approached by one photographer who offered to give us some copies of his pictures free of charge. Coral was so overwhelmed she invited him into the house for a coffee with our family and friends. He didn't ask a single question about April or attempt to pry any further into our lives, which really helped restore our faith in the media. We'll always be grateful for the restraint and respect he showed that day.

'It was a beautiful birthday and a great day,' I wrote in my diary that evening. 'It could so easily have been a very sad day but somehow it was turned around into a celebration of our beautiful daughter, who would have been six.

'Happy birthday April. I love you, beautiful, and miss you so much it hurts. All my love, Dad xxx.'

A few weeks later the search for April was officially called off. It had lasted nearly seven months. Some seventeen separate search teams, including specialised dog handlers, had hunted for April every week since she'd vanished. They'd covered around 60 square kilometres and 300 search sites, over some of the most challenging terrain in the UK. It had become the biggest ever police search in British history – but it still hadn't led us to April.

Despite this we'd developed a massive respect for the search teams. It had been a long, wet, cold winter but they'd been undeterred by the conditions, braving wind, rain and even snow in a bid to find what was left of our little girl. They'd only stopped during the Christmas period, resuming the search at the start of January. We'd often spot them going in and out of the town, never complaining about the task in hand.

The police had set up a feeding station for them on an industrial estate on the outskirts of Machynlleth, and for months Coral had been quietly making supplies for them. I'd often come home from a walk with the dogs to find her in the kitchen, making a huge plate of sandwiches or baking a chocolate cake. She'd then drive to the feeding station with a friend, where she'd hand over the food. As she's a fantastic cook and baker, the provisions were always gratefully received. It was our small way of saying thanks to the teams. We knew how desperate they were to find April. Sadly it wasn't to be.

Now, as the court case approached, we had to think about having a funeral with what scant remains we had. It was something we hoped we wouldn't have to face, but it was looking like it would be the reality of the situation. We couldn't make any arrangements until the trial was over, but we started to make tentative plans. We had a meeting with Kath Rodgers, the local vicar, and began to think about what kind of service we'd like. Coral said she wanted to have a white coffin and pink flowers, but I couldn't dwell on the details. How could we bury part of April when the rest of her was still out there somewhere?

'It's very difficult and awkward talking about funerals when we don't have a conviction or a body,' I wrote in my diary that evening. 'Is there no end to our suffering?

'We're so tired and so stressed. We don't know left from right, don't know which way is which. It's so confusing. I wonder what will be left of us when this is all done. The strain on me makes me feel sick and tired and Coral cries most of the day. I wonder if people realise what we're going through and just how tired and sad we are?

'You get sucked in and lose your way but really, as hard as it is, this is your moment, April, not ours. We have the rest of our lives and you have had yours taken away, so brutally, so cruelly. I feel our suffering is nothing in comparison to yours and I feel guilty for whinging and feeling sorry for myself.

'I miss you, April. Dad xxx.'

9

The Trial

The journey to Mold the night before the trial started was a quiet one. Melere came along with us and, again, she drove Coral in her car while I travelled with Dave. Coral and I felt sick with nerves. We got to our accommodation in the early evening but neither of us got much sleep. The next morning we felt drained as we walked past the cameras and into the court, where we were led to our seats at the right-hand side of the judge. In the end, the first day was a bit of an anticlimax. There were a few hours of legal argument, before a jury was selected and then it was time to go home.

I didn't sleep any better that night. Coral was unable to settle either and eventually I decided it would be better if I slept on the sofa for a few hours to give her a better chance of some rest. I knew there would be no chance of either of us sleeping while we both tossed and turned relentlessly.

In the early hours I found myself writing in my diary to pass the time. As sunlight began to stream through the windows, I was gripped by a feeling of dread and anticipation. This was the day the prosecution would open their case. The police and the Crown Prosecution Service had tried to prepare us as much as they could for what we were about to hear, but it didn't stop us worrying about how things would turn out.

What terrified me most was that there was only one person who really knew what happened to April that night and that, of course, was Mark Bridger. I couldn't help but fear that he held all the cards.

'We're all having a bad night's sleep,' I wrote. 'Coral is finding the bed hard and our minds are restless. Melere thinks there might be mice in the house. There is too much to think about. Even Dave and Hayley seem nervous, but I'm glad the trial has started now. Everyone will know what Mark Bridger did and we won't have to hide and keep quiet. I hope everyone gets the answers to their questions.'

We got to court around 10 a.m. and the jury was sworn in – nine women and three men. It felt strange knowing that the fate of the man who killed our daughter was in the hands of twelve strangers, but we knew we had a good case and we had to put our faith in them. There were so many reporters that there wasn't enough room in the main courtroom and some had to be sent to extra seats upstairs.

Once again, the morning was filled with legal argument and we had a long lunch before being called back in shortly after 2 p.m. Finally the court was ready for Elwen to open the case for the prosecution. I placed my hand in Coral's and closed my eyes tightly. I knew what we were about to hear would not be easy and this was only the beginning.

Again, Bridger was just a few feet away from us in the dock. I'd been trying not to look at him but now I couldn't help myself. He looked a lot less scruffy this time – he'd even put on a shirt and tie for the benefit of the jury. I hoped they wouldn't be fooled by his act.

Elwen cleared her throat and turned to face the jury. We knew how fierce her reputation was but now we were about to see her in action. We could only hope that her courtroom performance was as awe-inspiring as everyone promised us it would be.

'It's the defendant's case that he admits he drove April away,' Elwen said, eyeballing Bridger, as a hush fell on the room. We immediately sensed that when this woman spoke people listened.

'He admits that April is dead,' she went on. 'He admits that he killed her or *probably* killed her.

'He accepts he must have got rid of her body. He says that he does not know where April's body is, that he can't remember.'

She paused for effect, giving Bridger a stern glance. He refused to meet her eye and I hoped the jury could see how pathetic he looked.

'The prosecution case is this,' Elwen went on, 'that Mark Bridger abducted April, that he murdered her and that he went to great lengths to try and cover up what he had done. It's our case that the defendant's actions – abduction, murder, covering up what he has done – were sexually motivated.

'He has played, we say, a cruel game in pretending not to know what he has done to her. It's a game to try and save himself and try to manipulate his way out of full responsibility of what he has done.'

I breathed a sigh of relief, albeit a small one. If anyone could take Bridger down, it was Elwen.

She went on to speak of the evidence found on Bridger's computer. In the days before April was taken, checks had revealed he'd been obsessively searching for content related to child sex abuse and murder. Some of terms he'd used were 'nudism five-year-old' and 'British schoolgirl raped and murdered'. Coral had already turned white and I asked her if she needed a break.

'No, I'm staying for all of this,' she said, resolutely, although she was gripping my hand more tightly than before.

Elwen told the court that Bridger had downloaded images of various child murder victims, including Holly Wells and Jessica Chapman, the schoolgirls from Soham near Cambridge who were murdered by their school caretaker, Ian Huntley, in 2002. It made me want to vomit, but it didn't end there. Bridger also had cartoons depicting child rape and a folder full of pictures of local girls of all ages on his computer, including April and Jazmin. He'd apparently taken them from Facebook.

'That bastard,' I mumbled to myself, my stomach churning. My eyes fixed on him in the dock but he didn't dare look my way.

Elwen then said that, on the day April disappeared, Bridger's girlfriend, Vicky Fenner, had finished with him, and he'd sent Facebook messages to three local women.

'Hadn't realised you were single, as I am,' the first read. 'Do you fancy a drink or a club or even a meal? See how you feel.'

'Do you fancy a drink and a chat sometime?' said the second. 'No strings, OK?'

'Hi, would you like to go out for a meal or a drink?' read the final message.

I was almost shaking with rage, thinking of what disgusting thoughts would have been going through his mind.

Elwen briefly touched on some of the forensic evidence in her opening speech. For the first time, the details of the blood in the cottage and the bone fragments were made public. This was a huge weight off our shoulders. This was by far the most disturbing evidence we'd been told in confidence by the police and we'd been under a lot of strain, as we'd been forced to keep it to ourselves. Still, it didn't make it any easier hearing about it all over again and I felt an irrational sense of guilt. Surely there was something I could have done to protect April from this animal?

Elwen then described how April had been 'happy and smiling' as she'd got into Bridger's Land Rover but was never seen alive again. This was difficult, but not as difficult as hearing the 999 call Coral made just minutes later. As it was played to the court I felt the blood rush to my head, while cold goosebumps covered my body. Coral was ashen and continued to squeeze my hand. The court fell completely silent – I doubt any of the jury had ever heard anything so harrowing, and I'm sure some of them had tears in their eyes. Listening to Coral, panicked and breathless, barely able to speak, was horrendous, especially as we now knew how the events of that terrible night played out.

What really made us sick, however, was Bridger's reaction. He dabbed at his eyes, playing to the crowd, pretending to be upset as he heard my wife's choking sobs. I wanted to jump down from the public gallery and punch him. How dare he pretend to be moved by our distress?

'Crocodile tears,' Coral whispered hoarsely and I nodded. It was all I could do not to explode with rage. As I sat in my seat, bubbling with fury, I forced myself to think of April. I had to keep my dignity for her. We needed to do everything in our power to have this monster locked up and the key thrown away. Shouting and screaming and making a scene would only take the focus away from the case and from April.

None of us felt much like cooking that night, so we put some pizzas in the oven and had a quiet evening. My mind was still working overtime, so I stayed up while Coral and Melere had an early night. To pass the time, I jotted down my feelings about the day's events in my diary.

'It really worries me that Mark Bridger had pictures of April and Jazz,' I wrote. 'But what hurt the most was hearing the 999 call. It was so hard to listen to and made the hairs on my body stand up.

'We've had lots of lovely messages from people. We're just relieved everything is now coming out and we don't have to be so quiet or guarded with our words.

'April, I'm so sorry. No one deserves this but you're so special and beautiful. We love you and miss you.

'All our love, your family xxx.'

I was so exhausted, I managed to fall into a deep sleep as soon my head hit the pillow and I was relieved when Coral said she'd slept well, too. We got to court about 9.30 a.m. the next day, where my mum, Dai and Fil were waiting for us. They were allowed to stay with us in our little holding room and it was nice they'd come along to support us.

It proved to be another gruelling day. We were shown a slideshow of some of the indecent pictures found on Bridger's computer and I could tell this was getting a bit too much for Coral. I'd spent my most of my adult life cursing my poor eyesight but, on that day, I was actually thankful for it. Even from our front row seats, I couldn't make out any of the pictures properly, although I could see enough to appreciate how disgusting and depraved they were.

Elwen then went on to read out some of the statements made by Bridger to the police, one of which claimed he wanted to 'say sorry' to us because he'd run April over and killed her. Of course, we knew this was nonsense. If this had been a genuine accident, any decent person would have phoned for an ambulance straight away instead of leaving anything to chance. He then claimed to the police that he had got drunk and simply forgotten what he'd done with her body. It was preposterous that he thought this was believable.

'He was coming up with a story to try and explain away April's disappearance and his role in that,' Elwen told the jury. 'The prosecution case is that the defendant's account is a lie.'

Bridger shook his head and began to cry, with his head in his hands, but Elwen was quick to dismiss him.

'It appears lies and tears come easily to the defendant,' she said, brusquely. She then began to read from the statement Bridger had given to police shortly after he was arrested.

'It was an accident . . .' Elwen read the words slowly and clearly, her eyes boring into Bridger with every syllable. 'I crushed her with my car. I do not know where she is. As I was going to drive away, two girls on a bike came across me. I got out and saw one girl lying under my car. I did not abduct her. I did my best to revive her. I panicked. The more I drove through the night, the more I got pissed. My intention was to head to hospital. There was no life in her, no pulse, no breathing, no response. When my hand went over her chest, I knew there was more to it. I went numb. I did not know what I was doing.'

Coral was crying now. Even though we knew this wasn't what had happened, it was still hard to listen to.

'He didn't think he would have burned her or buried her or put her in the river,' Elwen told the jury, the disdain obvious in her voice. 'Being a father himself, he said he would not have done any of these things.'

Elwen then described how Bridger had been spotted the day after April was taken in a field near his home, carrying a black bin bag. He claimed he'd been in the field because he 'needed to go for a wee', despite his house being only a short distance away.

'We ask you, what was Mark Bridger doing at that location?' Elwen asked the jury. 'What was in that black binbag?'

I gripped Coral's hand but neither of us took our eyes off Bridger in the dock below.

Elwen recounted how police had searched Bridger's cottage half an hour before they'd arrested him. They'd hoped to find April, but instead they found evidence of a major clean-up operation.

'When they went in they stated that the house was uncomfortably hot,' she told the jury. 'There was a strong smell of detergents, a smell of cleaning products, air freshener and washed clothes.'

Elwen then went on to describe how Bridger had approached

other young girls from Machynlleth in the hours leading up to April's disappearance, even inviting one to his house for a 'sleep-over'. She also told the jury that forensic tests revealed that some of April's DNA had been found *inside of the crotch area of his tracksuit bottoms*. But before these tests had even been carried out, Bridger had attempted to cover himself. It was all so calculated; without prompting, he'd claimed he'd gone to the toilet after picking up April's body when she was crushed by his car because he knew there was a chance her DNA would be found on his genitals.

'This is a man who is forensically aware,' Elwen said. 'He knew how important it was from his point of view to try and get rid of any forensic evidence linking him to April.'

At that moment, Coral let go of my hand and ran out of the courtroom.

Coral recalls:

As the day went on, I found it harder and harder to listen to the evidence. The images found on Bridger's computer made me feel physically sick, so much so I could feel the bile rising in my throat. For once, I envied Paul and his poor sight.

I thought I'd want to shout out and call Bridger all of the names under the sun, to scream at him and tell him how much I hated him but, in reality, I didn't have the energy. All I could think about was April and what she must have suffered and it was slowly ripping me apart, bit by bit.

We'd been made aware of most of the content of Elwen's opening speech but I could hardly hold it together when she was making it. I struggled through hearing about the forensic evidence, Bridger's lies about how April had died and how he had callously cleaned his cottage from top to bottom to get rid of the evidence of her death. I told myself I was doing it for my daughter, otherwise I would have left within the first five minutes.

But when Elwen told the jury about April's DNA being found on the crotch area of his trousers, I couldn't take any more. I let go of Paul's hand, which I had been squeezing hard for the last few hours, and jumped out of my seat. Tears started to stream down my face and I could see all the reporters turning to look at me, but I didn't care. It was bad enough to know Bridger had killed my little girl in cold blood, for some sick, perverted thrill. But this final indignity – the idea of him sexually abusing our innocent five-year-old daughter – was too much to bear.

Paul, Dave and Hayley were close behind me but Hayley told Paul and Dave to go back into court while she calmed me down.

'How could he do it?' I sobbed. 'How could he do that to my little baby?'

Hayley soothed me for a few minutes, although there wasn't much she could say.

'I know I should have seen it coming,' I said. 'But it took me by surprise. It's just a bit too much, hearing about it all.'

'I know,' Hayley replied. 'Do you want to go back in? You don't have to if you don't want to.'

I knew I could have easily spent the rest of the day in our holding room, leaving Paul to hear the remaining evidence on his own, but I felt that would have been letting April down.

'No,' I said, wiping my tears away. 'Let's go back in.'

*

After court finished, we had a short meeting with Andy before Dave and Hayley drove us back to our cottage. My mum, Dai and Fil came with us. We all went out for a pub meal to try and take our minds off things, before my mum took me for a long walk. There was a lot to get our heads around, but we were trying our best.

'It's been a very emotional day,' I wrote, before I went to bed. 'Coral and I have struggled even though we knew some of this was coming.

'Andy talked to us about the day. We're happy with how things are going and so are the police. We all agreed that Mark Bridger just doesn't make sense in anything he says and that it's looking good for us so far.

'I love you, April. Dad xxx.'

The next day we had a day off from court, as the jury were being taken to Machynlleth to trace April's last steps. They were then driven to Ceinws to see Bridger's cottage. Bridger had waived his right to accompany them and we weren't surprised. We can only imagine how the people of Machynlleth would have reacted if they'd heard he was visiting the town.

We had a quiet day. Hayley took Coral, Melere and my mum to Chester shopping and afterwards we had a few games of pool and table tennis.

'It says on the news that the jury has been to Bryn-y-Gog, the town clock, the leisure centre and Ceinws where Mark Bridger lived,' I wrote. 'Today, I feel a lot better having had a rest. Coral seems good, too. I think she's relieved some things are now out in public. I am too.

'I love you, April. Dad xxx.'

*

On the Friday, Elwen read out a short statement from Jazmin, who had told the police that Bridger had sent her a friend request on Facebook shortly before April was taken. This sent shivers down my spine and we were relieved when court finished at lunchtime. This meant we could go home early for the weekend. Jazmin, Harley and the dogs were delighted to see us and it was good to be home. The weekend seemed to pass especially quickly and before we knew it was time to go back to Mold.

The May Bank Holiday traffic meant the roads were very busy and the journey took twice as long. By the time we got back to our accommodation, Coral had a bad stress headache and I was feeling sick with nerves. The reason we were so anxious was that Amy was due to take the stand the next day. She was the last person to see April alive and she had identified Bridger's vehicle. She was arguably the most important witness in the case and a conviction could potentially depend on what she said in court. It was a huge burden for a seven-year-old to bear.

Neither of us slept well, even when I moved into the spare room. When we got up, Coral was shaking violently and I wasn't faring much better.

Amy was to give evidence via video link from another room in the court. The judge, Mr Justice Griffith-Williams, Bridger's QC, Brendan Kelly, and Elwen all removed their wigs, so as not to intimidate her.

When Amy flashed up on the screen, she looked so small and vulnerable. She was hugging one of her teddies and wearing a T-shirt with the word 'love' emblazoned across it. Mr Justice Griffith-Williams was very patient with her. He tried to put her at ease by asking her teddy's name. Amy replied he was called Minty and the judge told her that Minty would look after her.

Amy was played a video of her police interview from the day after April was taken. Here, she described how she and April had been playing with Louise, but Louise's dad had told them they couldn't come into their house, as it was dinner time.

'We were going to go home and it was getting dark,' she said in the video. 'I said, "April, come on." I looked around and saw her by the Land Rover van. I saw her by the person who was waiting by the van.'

In the video, Amy said the Land Rover looked 'quite familiar', but she was surprised that April had got into it.

'The man didn't take her in the van,' she said. 'She got in the van with a happy face. She wasn't upset.'

The police officers in the video asked Amy some more questions and she said Bridger appeared to be 'waiting for someone', but she didn't think it was April.

'I think April wanted to go,' she said. 'I don't know why. Her mum and dad told her not to get into cars like that. The man didn't put her in the car. She wasn't crying; she was happy. The van just drove off. I didn't know she was going to get in the van.'

This was very difficult for Coral and me to hear, but we tried our best to keep it together. Amy was then cross-examined by Brendan Kelly. He was gentler with her than he would have been with an adult witness, but he was still quite forthright and I couldn't help but think his manner would have been a little unnerving for a small child. He suggested that Amy was lying – that she hadn't seen April getting into the car, that in fact she'd seen her being carried by Bridger after he'd run her over. But no matter how many times she was probed, Amy refused to crumble.

'She climbed over the back seat but the man didn't carry her,' she said, firmly.

'You've helped the court a great deal,' Mr Justice Griffith-Williams told her, after Brendan Kelly had finished. 'Off you go.'

Amy hugged her teddy and simply said: 'Thank you.'

I felt a wave of relief wash over me. Amy had been amazing, far stronger than we'd ever expected. She hadn't buckled under the pressure of cross-examination, which is more that can be said for some adults. It seemed that almost everyone – including Bridger's lawyer – had underestimated her.

The next witness was Amy's mum. She said that when she asked Amy what had happened, Amy said she had told April not to get into the vehicle but that April replied that she would be 'fine'. My stomach knotted at the thought of April's lovely, child-like innocence. She was so sweet-natured, trusting of everyone she met, and completely unaware of the evils the world held. It wouldn't have entered her head that the man she'd encountered on that fateful autumn night could have done her any harm. Bridger was a callous predator and I could feel my hatred for him pumping through my veins as he sat in front of me, consumed by pathetic self-pity.

On the way back to our cottage that evening, Dave told us that the guards watching Bridger had nicknamed him 'Tiny Tears' because he was always crying and saying he couldn't cope with being in prison.

'He'd better bloody get used to it,' I said. Now Amy's evidence had gone so well I was feeling much more confident of a conviction. We didn't want to take anything for granted, but it was becoming harder to see how the jury could continue to buy Bridger's lies, if they ever had done.

'Amy was a star today,' I wrote that night. 'She did very well. Brendan Kelly, Mark Bridger's barrister, asked her a lot of questions but she told it as it was. Amy's mum was also a witness and she did very well too.

'Both Coral and I feel better now Amy has finished her evidence. We feel she was badgered a bit by Kelly but she spoke truly and we are very impressed by her. It was hard listening to her, especially when she said April went into Mark Bridger's car on her own with a happy face.

'I feel a lot better. I can't see how he can get out of this now.

'I love you, April. Dad xxx.'

The rest of the second week passed uneventfully. On one morning there was a fire alarm, which was particularly stressful for Coral, as she still wasn't good at dealing with crowds, but Dave took us out in the car for half an hour, which helped calm her down. The prosecution also called some police witnesses and plotted Bridger's movements on the day April disappeared. This was quite hard to follow and took its toll on both of us. Although this evidence hadn't been as tough for us to hear as some of the information already put before the court, I still could find myself in tears without a moment's notice. Both Coral and I found it impossible to tell when the emotion of it all would hit us – all we knew was that we'd feel paralysed by grief when it did.

'I cried myself to sleep last night,' I wrote, one morning before

Dave and Hayley collected us. 'It just piles up on me and I have to cry. Court is stressful and very tiring but it seems like things are looking good for our case.

'I love you, April. Dad xxx.'

As ever, coming home at the weekend was hard, knowing April wouldn't be there to greet us. It had been my mum's turn to watch Jazmin and Harley and we were relieved when she told us that they'd both been well behaved.

A few friends dropped by over the course of the evening to see how we were doing. All of them remarked on how strong we seemed as a couple and how, no matter what was thrown at us, we faced it together. Until now, Coral and I had been muddling through, doing what we could to keep our heads above water. Often, the strain would get to us and we'd have a small spat or a few cross words and we'd both feel worse until we made up. It almost hadn't occurred to me that this was completely natural and that we were actually doing much better than most couples in our position. I remembered the frightening statistics I'd heard about marriage break-ups following the murder of a child, but they only made me more determined than ever to keep fighting for what Coral and I had. Through the eyes of others, I could see that we were two halves of a whole – there was no way either of us could have ever faced this torment alone.

Coral was exhausted so, when the last of our impromptu visitors left, she headed off to bed, as Jazmin and Harley watched a film upstairs. I, too, was feeling very weary but I wanted to write in my diary before I caught up on my sleep.

'That's the second week over,' I wrote. 'It's going fast. It's very emotional. When you stop, you just feel so tired. It's hard to concentrate and operate as a normal person. I find small things can upset me and I get stressed very quickly. Coral is the same and we can both be snappy and, at times, a little bad-tempered.

'It's nice to be home but it does all come back to us – everything reminds us of April. Coral does seem better at home, though. I think she needs to be close to Jazz and Harley and amongst friends. I feel very tired and tearful – I nearly always feel tearful these days. I just don't have a purpose or a goal in life. I just want my girl back – to hear her laugh and sing in the garden, to put her to bed and listen to her talk, to kiss her on the head and tell her I love her and hear her say it back with that beautiful, Welsh voice.

'A few friends have dropped by to say hello and they've all said that we are doing so well and that we are a strong and amazing couple. I feel a little embarrassed but also proud they think this.

'I love you, April. Dad xxx.'

We travelled back to Mold on the Sunday night in preparation for court on the Monday. We'd been told this week was likely to focus mainly on the forensic evidence found in Bridger's cottage.

First we heard evidence from Emma Howes, a forensic scientist from Birmingham, who had examined Bridger's house as part of the investigation. As we expected, she confirmed that the blood found in the flat was a match for April's DNA and the chances of it belonging to someone else were a billion to one. We already knew that traces of our daughter's blood had been found all over the flat, but we both found it hard to listen when the witness said that the puddle on the living room floor suggested April's little body had been lying by the fire 'for some time', as the blood had soaked through to the underside of the carpet. She then spoke about the traces of blood found in the hallway, saying this indicated a pattern of 'dripped blood'.

Emma Howes was a very matter-of-fact witness and I was a little surprised by how easily she could speak about the scene of this horrific crime without becoming upset or emotional. I had to remind myself that she was simply being professional, not insensitive, and that we needed the opinion of experts like her if we wanted to convict Bridger.

She said that, in her opinion, the blood was 'diluted', suggesting someone had attempted to clean it up. This was a little too much for Coral and she had to go outside for a five-minute break at one point, but she steeled herself and was soon back in to hear the rest of the evidence.

On the Tuesday of the third week we heard from another forensic scientist, a man from Edinburgh called Roderick Stewart. He told the court he had spent two days thoroughly examining the Land Rover but had found no evidence that Bridger had knocked April over.

'If there had been a collision between the Land Rover and a person or bike there would be evidence,' he told Elwen. 'It always leaves a trace, whether it be scratches or dents on an object such as a car or bike.

'This vehicle weighs two tonnes – it's going to do a lot of damage. My conclusion, based on forty years' experience, shows no damage to the vehicle. Nothing on the underside, nothing on the bodywork and nothing on the wheels.'

I couldn't help but glance at Bridger during Roderick Stewart's

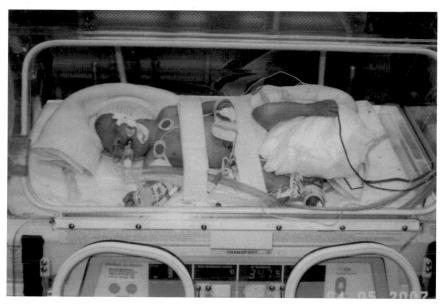

Our little fighter. When April was born she weighed only 4lbs 2oz but with our love and care she grew into a smiley baby.

Aged seven months, April was already showing her character.

April at school, aged four.

The Jones family in happier times, 2011. Left to right: Jazmin, Harley, Paul, April and Coral.

Coral with April and Harley.

A father's love. Paul with April.

April's last Christmas, aged four.

© Rob Formstone 2015

Members of the public queue at the Bro Ddyfi Leisure Centre to sign up to be part of the search for April on the night she went missing, 1 October 2012.

Police divers and HM Coastguard carry one of the dinghies to the Dyfi River on day six of the search.

© Rob Formstone 2015

Machynlleth clock tower was adorned with pink ribbons throughout the search for April.

Day five. Mid-Wales, West Wales and Shropshire Fire and Rescue Services were involved in the search of the Dyfi River near Dyfi Bridge at Macynlleth.

HM Coastguard and North Wales fire service crew scour the banks of the river Dyfi, with the RNLI inshore lifeboat from Aberdovey searching the river itself.

April missing – days five, six and seven. Specialist sonar equipment was brought in to search the Dyfi River.

Coral and Paul in April's bedroom, left as it was the day she disappeared. Photo taken approximately a year after April went missing.

Harley in thought by the sea on day spent with family liaison officers.

The fence of ribbons where Paul, on his daily walk with the dogs, tied a pink ribbon for every day April was missing.

Paul and Coral, flanked by family liaison officers Dave Roberts and Hayley Heard, arrive at Mold Crown Court to attend the trial of Mark Bridger.

Public church service and procession for April on Sunday, day six of the search in and around Macynlleth.

April's funeral. The horse-drawn hearse makes its way down Macynlleth main street followed by hundreds of mourners.

Jazz Jones, April's sister, and mum Coral with the special April balloon, released to celebrate what would have been her sixth birthday, 6 April 2013.

Family and friends release the balloons.

Paul and Coral's April tattoos, representing their love and a constant reminder of the daughter they lost.

April's 'hugging tree', set on a quiet side of the mountain above Macynlleth. It was covered in crocheted pink squares made by friends, family and members of the public.

evidence. He was now sitting in the dock with his head in his hands, in tears. This time I didn't doubt the tears were real but they weren't for April, they were for himself. He was beginning to realise just how bleak things were looking for him.

Roderick Stewart then went on to say that he'd examined both April and Amy's bikes and had still found no evidence of a collision, telling the jury that the only damage he could find was from wear and tear.

Brendan Kelly was given the opportunity to cross-examine the witness and he asked why he hadn't carried out any investigations near the garages on Bryn-y-Gog, where Bridger claimed the collision had taken place.

'There wouldn't have been any point,' Roderick Stewart replied. 'There had not been a collision. There wouldn't have been anything to see.'

Bridger's case was unravelling before our eyes. It was the only thing that made listening to the evidence seem worthwhile.

'I can't wait until he takes the stand,' Coral said, when we were back at our cottage that night. 'I want to watch him squirm.'

'It has been stressful, what with all the talk of April's blood here and there as if it was just casual talk,' I wrote that night. 'Coral found it very hard but she's very strong and recovers fast. I've prepared myself for the worst case scenario, so it doesn't come as such as shock, but it still hurts and makes me sick to my boots.

'I still can't understand how a father could do such a thing to our April. She was so special and beautiful, full of life and courage, what with her pain in her legs.

'I love you, April. Dad xxx.'

*

While this was all going on, we also had to contend with the press interest in the case. Coral and I had received countless letters from newspapers, magazines and television programmes, asking if we would be interested in doing an interview after the verdict had been announced. We hadn't ruled this out – in fact, we were keen to pay tribute to April in our own words and to give our side of the story. After all, we had spent months being silent and dignified for the sake of a fair trial. Nonetheless, justice for our little girl remained our absolute priority and we asked the journalists who had contacted us to allow us to focus on the case before we made a decision. Most were very respectful, with the exception of one.

Perhaps we were a little bit naive. We were unwittingly at the centre of probably the biggest story of the year, but we were so wrapped up in the court case that we didn't realise that the media were falling over themselves to secure an exclusive with us once the trial was over. I'd given this journalist my personal mobile number but, in the midst of the distressing forensic evidence, had asked him not to contact us until the following week when I would hopefully be in a better frame of mind to speak to him. Unfortunately, he wouldn't take no for an answer, and I had to switch my mobile off to avoid being disturbed by his calls.

Rhian, the police press manager, then told us the same journalist had contacted her several times and had been quite rude when asking to speak to us. In the end, Coral called him with Hayley's help and asked him to leave us alone. I understand this man was probably under a lot of pressure to get the story but the irony of it all was that we'd probably have given him the exclusive if he'd just been a bit more sensitive to our needs.

'We have no time for this distraction,' I wrote in my diary. 'He just didn't listen and wouldn't take no for an answer. He even denied ringing the police. I hope he will now stop and respect our wishes.'

Towards the end of the week, we heard more evidence from Mark Bridger's police interviews. By now, it was beginning to become obvious just how much of a fantasist he was. Paul Hobson, Elwen's junior barrister, read out some transcripts from when Bridger was first arrested. He'd made up so many stories to try and worm his way out of the awful situation he'd created. Each one was more incredible than the last. Firstly he insisted he could not have abused April because he was virtually impotent. Next he told officers that he'd been looking at the vile images found on his computer because he wanted to study the development of his own children. When this didn't seem to wash, he said he was carrying out an investigation into the availability of child pornography and that he'd been so outraged by what he found that he'd written to several internet providers to complain.

I shifted uncomfortably in my seat, as Paul Hobson read out part of the transcript in which Bridger said he'd had a 'mental block' and had no idea what he'd done with April.

'"When you came in before and said you were arresting me for murder, I was initially relieved,"' Paul said, reading from the papers he was holding. Bridger put his head in his hands as his words were repeated to the jury. '"At that point, I honestly thought you'd found her. I don't know where she is. In my mind, I've obviously put her somewhere and I can't get that back."'

'"I would like to say to Paul and Coral, I never meant for this to happen. I never meant to put them through this. I've got kids of my own; I have known them for years."'

His words were hollow but what was most chilling was how he had reacted to a sighting of himself in his car, at the war monument in the town, around ten minutes after April was taken. A witness had seen him stop for a minute or so before driving off towards Ceinws. He claimed he was driving around in a panic because he'd run April over and that he'd stopped 'to think about what to do'. I put my arm around Coral and gritted my teeth to try and control the tidal wave of grief and anger that had engulfed me.

We both knew in our hearts that Bridger hadn't stopped to think about what to do with April's lifeless body. April had still been alive and he'd stopped to make a final decision as to whether or not to go through with the horrific crime he'd been plotting. I don't know what he had to consider; perhaps he weighed up the risk of being caught and wrongly assumed he could get away with it. All I know is that, when he drove off, he let go of every shred of humanity in his body.

In the interviews, Bridger was also asked about his background. Everyone in Machynlleth knew how proud he was of his alleged army career, but it was quickly becoming apparent that this was nothing more than a product of his imagination. He claimed he'd cheated death several times, that he was shot in the back while on duty with the army, and that he'd served all over the world, everywhere from Afghanistan to Belize. He also said he broke several bones in his back when a parachute jump went wrong. As ridiculous as it sounds, this brought a little light relief. I could see some of the jury giggling and, at one point, I had to cover my mouth to stop myself from laughing out loud. Dave bowed his head because he couldn't keep a straight face and even the judge looked amused. It was obvious that this pathetic excuse for a human being, crying like a baby in the dock, had never been anywhere near a war zone.

Still, Coral and I were left feeling very drained and wondering how we'd get through another week and a half of evidence.

'I've found it very hard listening to Mark Bridger's statement,' I wrote that night. 'He is going on about April and how he crushed her little body and tried in vain to bring her back, then telling us how he drank so much vodka and cider he can't remember what he did with her body – it makes me feel sick. It's taken a lot out of me, much more than I expected.

'I don't know how Coral and I will manage next week when he takes the stand and tries to convince the jury of what a lovely guy he is, when really he's a bastard. I'm really worried about what it will do to Coral.

'I love you, April. Dad xxx.'

That weekend I felt I needed some time to myself, so on the Saturday morning I walked up my hill and tied a ribbon to the fence. Most of the ribbons were now looking a little weather-beaten. Some were frayed at the edges and their colour had faded to a pale pink or white shade. I sat on top of the hill for a long time that day, watching the bows flutter sadly in the wind.

'Oh, April,' I wept. 'I'll never get to see you or hear you again.'

Later on, Tim called round and asked if I wanted to go to the leisure centre. I felt better for a few hours in the gym and, afterwards, we had a swim and a sauna, which really helped revitalise me.

The Sunday was a beautiful, sunny day and Harley and Jazmin had a water fight with some of the neighbours. It was lovely to see them having fun, but Coral and I couldn't help but feel low.

'April would have loved this,' Coral sighed.

'I know,' I replied, blinking back tears.

Sue had come down from Holyhead to look after the children, so she and Coral went to bingo while I took the dogs for a walk and caught up with my diary.

'No matter what I do, I just come back to thinking of April,' I wrote. 'It's good just to be normal for a while but now I feel so down and upset. I'm a bit battered and faded, just like the ribbons on the hill.

'I love you, April. Dad xxx.'

Dave and Hayley agreed to take us to court on Monday morning from Machynlleth to give us some extra time at home, but neither of us slept well. It was another exhausting day, as the evidence yet again focused on the images found on Bridger's computer.

On the Tuesday, both the prosecution and the defence called expert witnesses to give their opinions on the bone fragments found in the wood burner. The prosecution witnesses were Professor Cattaneo and Dr Julie Roberts, a leading forensic anthropologist and archaeologist. Dr Roberts took the stand first and told the court she had been asked to take three things into consideration when examining the fragments: whether or not they were burnt bone, whether or not they were human, and where in the skeleton they were from.

She was given five fragments and concluded that at least four of them contained features unique to a human skull. She said she believed the skull was that of a younger individual, possibly a child aged between four and eight. She added that the reason she could not obtain a DNA profile was because the pieces of bone had been so badly burned.

As part of the investigation, the fragments had been taken to the School of Veterinary Medicine in Liverpool and compared with those of fourteen other species, including dogs, cats, foxes and chickens. Dr Roberts remained convinced that the fragments had come from a child.

Professor Cattaneo, whose work mainly focused on studying the badly burned remains of organised crime victims in Italy, then gave the results of her findings. She agreed with Dr Roberts, that the pieces of bone were most likely the remains of a human being.

However, when Brendan Kelly called his own witness to the stand, we weren't sure what to expect. Professor Sue Black, from Dundee University in the north-east of Scotland, was a world-famous anthropologist, who had previously given evidence in many high-profile murder trials and had been awarded an OBE for her forensic work in Kosovo. She told the jury she was not confident that the fragments found were from a human skull. She claimed the other experts were guilty of 'confirmation bias' – that they'd simply been looking for evidence to support a theory they'd already decided was true.

'I have not seen anything like that in a human skeleton,' she replied, when questioned on the fragments. 'I have no idea what it could be. If you are going to look for faces in the clouds, you will find them, but it does not mean that they are fact and that they exist.'

I was a little unnerved. This woman was obviously a very respected scientist and, without a body, the forensic evidence was the cornerstone of our case. But Elwen was more than a match for her and, during her cross-examination, managed to get Professor Black to agree there was at least a possibility these fragments had come from April, although Professor Black insisted she still had to 'sit on the fence' and refused to confirm there was any scientific evidence that these were our daughter's remains. When Elwen finished grilling her, I felt slightly more relaxed. I just hoped this testimony hadn't planted too big a seed of doubt in the minds of the jurors.

The next morning, Brendan Kelly would call Bridger as his second witness. Coral and I slept surprisingly well, but we were anxious about the day ahead.

Bridger was brought to the stand in handcuffs by two guards but the jury were not allowed to see him like this, so he was released before they were brought in. It was strange, seeing him let loose on the stand. His voice broke when he took the oath. Coral and I stared straight at him.

His barrister asked him a few questions about his background and why he'd lied about being in the army. His voice was small and pathetic as he responded.

'When I moved to the Machynlleth area people always wanted to know who I was, where I was from, my past, my present,' he replied. 'I had always been interested in the military so I just said I am ex-military and people took that as what I did.'

He was then asked about the photographs. I could see the

colour draining from Coral's face when he spoke about Jazmin and how pretty he thought she was. It made my skin crawl.

His barrister then went on to talk about the incident itself and he repeated the same lies we'd been hearing for weeks. Despite the mountain of forensic evidence Elwen and her team had gathered against him, he continued to claim he'd run April over and had forgotten what he'd done with her body. He even claimed the bones in the fire were from a chicken he'd cooked for his children the weekend before April disappeared. It was like he hadn't listened to a word that had been said since the trial had begun. I think he'd got to the stage where he actually believed his own lies.

'I still do not recall having little April in my car,' he repeated. Without warning, Coral stood up and ran out of the courtroom, her hand clapped to her face.

Coral recalls:
Little April ... these were the words we'd always used to describe our youngest daughter, full of love and affection. When I heard them spring from Mark Bridger's lips, I felt like someone had stabbed me hard in the heart and was slowly twisting the knife.

How dare he call my daughter little April? People who loved her called her little April. It was too much to bear. I stood against the wall and sobbed. He was so brazen, putting on a show like this for the jury. Pretending he cared, pretending he was crying for April when really his tears were for no one but himself.

My face was hot and my already weak legs had turned to jelly. I knew I had to steady myself, to go back in and face the monster who had robbed me of my child but I needed a few minutes to get myself together.

Hayley followed me out. She put a supportive hand on my arm and told me to take my time to compose myself.

'I'm fine,' I sobbed. 'I'm fine. I just need a minute.'

He was probably enjoying my agony. He probably got a kick out of seeing me running out of court in tears. I wondered how he would feel if he had to live my life for a day if this had happened to one of his children. But it was useless. Bridger was a callous, disgusting animal. He didn't have emotions like Paul and me.

I took a deep breath.

'I'm ready to go back in,' I said to Hayley, dabbing the last of my tears.

'Are you sure?' she asked.

'Yes,' I replied, firmly. 'I want him to sit and look at me. He's not getting away with anything.'

I sat back down in my seat at the front of the court. Clasping Paul's hand, I fixed my gaze on Bridger once again.

He was still saying those words.

Little April, little April, little April . . .

It seemed like he dropped the phrase in every few sentences, just to see how I'd react. I had no real idea if he'd sensed that this was what had made me so upset, but in the heat of the moment I became convinced he was doing it purely to torment me.

'How can he call her little April?' I raged to Paul when the court was adjourned for a short break. 'She was *our* little April. He's got no bloody right.'

*

It had been a distressing day, particularly for Coral, but when Brendan Kelly had finished with Bridger, Elwen had the chance to cross-examine him. She didn't pull any punches and got straight to the point.

'Where is April?' she demanded of him.

'I don't know,' he replied, fighting back tears. 'I really don't know.'

'What did you do with April's body?' she said.

'I don't know,' he answered. The panic was evident in his voice and it was almost fun for us to watch him squirm.

'You have absolutely no idea?' Elwen asked. 'Is that what you are telling the jury? Can you just consider the scale and scope of the police search?'

Bridger said nothing, simply looking at the floor.

'You have heard the evidence,' Elwen went on, sternly. 'Can you agree, whatever you did with April's body, you got rid of her so thoroughly that no part of her, apart from possibly the blood and bone, has been found? Do you agree?'

'I'm not proud of it,' Bridger replied.

'Well, you did it,' Elwen retorted.

She then moved on to the duct tape found in the dashboard of the car. One of the cartoons he'd viewed in the hours before April went missing showed a young girl being held down by a man and restrained by duct tape. Elwen asked him if he remembered this.

'I don't know,' he replied yet again, blinking back more tears.

We went back to our cottage that night knowing Elwen had a full day to finish her cross-examination the next day. I couldn't sleep. I kept thinking of Bridger and his lies.

'Elwen just ripped Mark Bridger to bits,' I wrote in my diary in the early hours. 'She only had an hour with him but he looked stupid. Not one person believes a word he says. He lied the whole time but I just wish he'd own up. We all know he murdered April and burned her in the fire but he intends to keep going. I just hope Elwen makes him snap and then we'll know for definite.

'I love you, April. Dad xxx.'

We left for court around 9 a.m. Melere came with us but we were all quiet. We knew the day ahead would be tense.

Elwen began by grilling Bridger about the child pornography on his computer. She had to ask him five times if he had viewed the images before he cracked and admitted it, but still the lies kept coming. Bridger insisted he hadn't meant to search for an image of a naked five-year-old girl, but a naked fifteen-year-old girl. It was all, he claimed, because he wanted to check his teenage daughter was developing properly.

'Are you a paedophile?' Elwen asked him over and over.

'No,' he answered. 'It was a mis-type. I was looking into the development of my two youngest children.'

Bridger then repeated the lie that he'd kept the images to complain to internet providers.

'Are you saying you had this disgusting filth on your computer to complain to companies?' Elwen asked, narrowing her eyes in his direction.

Bridger screwed up his eyes before he answered. 'A small batch of pictures, yes,' he said. He then claimed he wasn't a paedophile because he didn't spend every day looking at 'reams and reams' of indecent images. Elwen replied that he didn't have to look at them constantly to be a paedophile.

'Yes you do,' he insisted. 'You have to have serious problems.'

I could tell this was becoming hard for Coral, who was quite tearful, but she knotted her fingers through mine and stayed rooted to her seat.

Elwen then moved on to the pictures of the other murder victims, asking Bridger why he had stored images of Holly Wells and Jessica Chapman.

'I had read the stories and the sad story of the two young victims of Soham,' he said. 'I had read crime stories for many years. They were not all rapes and murders, there are also images of real-life accidents. These are not all crimes and rapes and paedophilia.'

After lunch, Elwen focused on what Bridger had done with April's body after he'd abducted her. By this point, he was on the verge of hysteria.

'I had a dead child in my car!' he said, almost shouting, as his sobs got louder. 'How does that affect anyone? I had pins and needles. I felt sick and frightened.'

At several points, the judge had to tell Bridger to answer the questions put to him, instead of trying to argue with Elwen. He was a desperate man.

Elwen then asked why traces of April's blood had been found on his living room floor. He replied that he'd laid her body in front of the fireplace to 'keep her warm'.

'She was dead, and in some silly way it would have been some peace and quiet for her,' he added. He was still crying his vile tears of self-pity. 'Maybe it was because it would be warm for her.'

'Do you accept you killed April?' Elwen said.

'No. I caused the death of April,' he replied. 'I did not kill her. I did not dispose of her body. Disposed is such a horrible word.'

It had been a draining day, but it wasn't over yet. When court finished shortly after 4 p.m., Elwen said she would need to cross-examine Bridger further in the morning. We wanted her to do all she could to see him sent down, but we were at breaking point and I wasn't sure how much more Coral could take. She'd tried to be strong all day, but the exhaustion was evident on her face.

'Elwen made a fool of Mark Bridger again today,' I wrote. 'He just kept on talking but the tension never left us all day. It's been a difficult day, listening to a desperate man who will do anything to get out of his predicament. Coral is in bits and very stressed. I'm OK because I know what's he's done. I've known for a long time, so I'm just listening to his sad attempts to get out of his mess.

'I love you, April. Dad xxx.'

Thankfully the rest of Elwen's cross-examination took only an hour or so. She quizzed Bridger on what he'd done with April's body and this was overwhelming for Coral. We went out of court for around twenty minutes and when we came back in the cross-examination had been completed. We were glad it was over and that we didn't have to hear any more of Bridger's pathetic lies.

The judge then told us the lawyers would be able to begin their closing speeches the following Tuesday, as Monday was another bank holiday. The jury was expected to go out on Wednesday.

Coral fell into my arms and we both cried a few tears of relief. The end was in sight.

*

When Dave and Hayley picked us up on Tuesday morning, we were all on edge. There wasn't much conversation. We'd come such a long way and we couldn't even consider the prospect of a not guilty verdict.

We were surprised by how concise Elwen's speech was. She managed to condense four weeks of evidence into an hour and a half. Both Coral and I were tearful as she spoke, especially when she mentioned little Amy.

'April's little friend has been one of the most impressive witnesses, all seven years of her,' she told the jury. 'The totality of her evidence is powerful and compelling in this case.

'Imagine the frustration for the defendant that in effect his whole story is laid to waste by the evidence of a seven-year-old girl? If you conclude that she is telling the truth then that is the end of the defendant's lies, fabrication, fantasy.

'On his own admission, this is a man who over twenty years ago decided to create a whole new lie – a whole new life for himself, and a man who was prepared to live that lie.

'He came up with a false identity, embroidered the fabricated fantasy that he had been a soldier of some skill, a mercenary of some skill. It was a story he advanced for his own benefit and it was a lie that was advanced to everyone. You have seen some glimpses into his mindset and some of those glimpses, you may have thought, are quite frankly shocking.

'The evidence points to one and only one conclusion and that is this defendant, Mark Bridger, is guilty of counts one, two and three of the indictment.'

We had a short break for lunch, before Brendan Kelly began his closing speech. We found this easier to listen to, mainly because it had far less substance than Elwen's. He asked the jury not to base their verdict on speculation and told them that Bridger was not necessarily guilty of April's abduction and murder simply because child pornography had been found on his computer. We appreciate this man had a job to do, but he was quite clearly clutching at straws.

That evening I saw little point in going to bed. I sat on the sofa, thinking and crying, while Coral tried to get some rest. When we went back to court in the morning, more cameras than usual were thrust in our faces as we approached the entrance. The judge spent a few hours giving the jury some legal guidance.

'You're under no pressure for time,' he told the jurors. 'You must take as long as you need and no verdict should be based on guesswork.'

Shortly after 1 p.m., they retired to consider their verdict.

'This is it,' I said to no one in particular, clutching Coral's hand.

Around 4 p.m., we were told to go home for the night. The jury had not yet reached a decision, but were expected to have done so by the next day.

It was hard to imagine how we would get through the next few hours. Thankfully a few friends from Machynlleth had come up to visit us and they suggested going out for a pub meal. A nail technician also came round to give Coral a manicure, which perked her up a bit.

Over dinner and a few beers, we managed to unwind a little, although our minds never wandered far from what the next day had in store for us. The case against Bridger was so compelling it was hard to see how he could be acquitted but it didn't stop us worrying about it. Dave and Hayley had told us never to take anything for granted, and the thought of our daughter's killer roaming the streets again was unbearable. I was certain it would kill Coral and I didn't have much faith that I'd fare any better.

'The tension was massive today,' I wrote in my diary that night. 'You can really feel it. Minutes feel like hours. We're all hoping tomorrow the jury will come back with the verdict we want. This is all for you, April.

'We all love you and miss you. Dad xxx.'

10

The Verdict

On the morning of Thursday 30 May 2013, the alarm woke Coral and me up at 6.45 a.m. We sat up in bed with a start and were both surprised how well we'd slept considering what the day ahead held. I left Coral to get ready while I popped downstairs to make us breakfast and coffee. Already I could feel my body tensing with nerves as I fixed my pink bow to my freshly ironed shirt.

Dave and Hayley picked us up just after 9 a.m. This time, Rhian, the police press manager, was in the car with them and she gave us some advice on speaking to the media after the verdict was announced. In the event of a guilty verdict, she said she would help Coral draft a statement to read out on the court steps.

It was all becoming very real.

A few of our friends had gathered at court, as well as my mum,

Dai and Fil, who had brought Jazmin along with them. We'd never have allowed her to sit through the trial, as it would have been extremely disturbing for her, but we agreed that she could be in court to hear the verdict. By now, she was just a few months shy of her eighteenth birthday and Coral and I felt she was mature enough to attend the final day of the trial. We also hoped it might help her understand the court process and what we'd been doing for the past month.

Coral and I walked through the sea of flashbulbs and into the court, where we took our seats. The jurors filed in one by one and confirmed, as we'd expected, that they needed more time to continue their deliberations.

We were taken to our holding room, where the volunteers made us some hot drinks. I could barely taste my coffee. It was hard to know how to feel. On the one hand, a guilty verdict was what we'd been hoping and praying for these last eight months, but it was always going to be a bittersweet moment – and it wouldn't bring April back.

I smiled to myself as I watched Dave and Hayley. They'd always been so calm and cool but today neither of them could sit still for a minute, fidgeting with their phones and pacing the floor. They'd been with us every step of the way on this terrible journey and the result mattered almost as much to them as it did to us.

'Look at them,' I said to Coral. 'They're like yo-yos.'

There was nothing we could do but wait. Every minute seemed like an hour as we drank endless cups of tea and coffee and watched every second on the clock.

'They can't take much longer,' I said, as I too began to pace up and down the small room, but in truth I had no idea how long the jury would deliberate for. For all we knew, we could be waiting days.

Finally, just after noon, the jury bell sounded and we were summoned back to the court. It had been just over two hours since we'd arrived at court but it felt like years.

'Is this it?' I asked Dave.

'It could be,' he said, wringing his hands, nervously. 'But they could just ask a question, or be looking for a break.'

I hoped it wasn't the latter. The longer the deliberations went on, the more nervous I became. It goes without saying that the longer the jury is out, the greater chance there is of a not guilty verdict. I was utterly convinced the prosecution had proved Bridger's guilt beyond reasonable doubt, but what if the jury wasn't? What if there was one rogue juror who wasn't quite satisfied that the evidence was enough to convict him? What if there was someone who actually believed his lies and thought he was innocent? It was almost too much to bear.

We filed back into our seats, with Dave and Hayley on either side of us. The courtroom was so quiet I was convinced everyone would be able to hear the sound of my heart hammering in my chest.

Mr Justice Griffith-Williams came in first, before the court clerk summoned Bridger to the dock. Then the jury entered, shuffling into their seats one by one.

After what seemed like an eternity, the judge spoke.

'Have you reached a verdict?' he asked the jury spokesman.

'Yes,' the spokesman replied, rising from his seat. He handed an envelope to the judge, who opened it, read its contents and nodded. It was impossible to gauge his reaction to what he'd just seen.

Then, the court clerk asked the spokesman for the jury's verdict on the first charge on the indictment, that of April's abduction. My knuckles were white as I squeezed Coral's hand as hard as I could, but I barely registered when the word 'guilty' passed his lips. It was the next verdict we were all waiting on.

'In relation to charge two on the indictment, the murder of April Jones, how do you find the defendant?' the clerk asked.

'Guilty,' the spokesman replied. He added that the verdict had been unanimous.

'Yes!' was all Coral could say. 'Yes!'

Bridger nodded his head and appeared to swallow hard. The spokesman was then asked for the jury's verdict on the charge of perverting the course of justice by disposing of April's body and again he replied that the jury had found Bridger guilty.

Just then, something quite extraordinary happened. To my right, Dave put his head in his hands and began to sob audibly. It was such a strange sight, to see this tough, resilient man crying like a schoolboy in public but I knew his tears had come straight from the heart. He had been our rock, so collected throughout everything, never betraying the strain the case was having on him.

On Coral's side, Hayley was even more emotional than Dave – she too was openly weeping and seemed powerless to stop the tears streaming down her face. Both of our FLOs had been so strong for so long. It was only then I realised how much of themselves they'd given us, how they'd put their lives on hold for many months to make sure this moment arrived. We'd almost forgotten that they were both parents themselves and this, of course, was every parent's worst nightmare. Hayley later admitted that, as a mother, she had put herself in Coral's shoes many times over.

Perhaps the feelings they'd been bottling up for the past eight months had now finally come to the surface.

Strangely enough, the emotion of it took a few minutes to hit Coral and me. Neither of us was crying. I wrapped my arms around Jazmin, who had tears in her eyes, but I think I was in shock.

The judge said he would sentence Bridger at 2 p.m. The court was then adjourned as we were ushered back to our holding room, where Rhian was waiting for us. She, too, was in tears. It was only then that Coral sank into my arms and allowed herself to cry a little. But she quickly composed herself and wiped her eyes. There would be plenty of time for that later and we still had the sentencing to get through.

The next few minutes passed in a blur as police officers and court officials hugged and wept on each other's shoulders. It was only now that we could see how much this verdict meant to so many people. We couldn't begin to express how grateful we were to each and every individual who'd worked so hard to make it happen.

Rhian and Hayley helped Coral draft a statement to read on the court steps once Bridger had been sentenced, and she practised it a few times. I could tell she was nervous – it was a wonder she could speak at all.

Just under two hours later, Coral, Jazmin and I were summoned back into the court, with Dave and Hayley at either side of us. The jury was free to go, as their duties had been completed, but the judge had asked the jurors if they would like to see Bridger sentenced. We were very touched when all twelve of them returned, taking their seats for one final time.

I stared hard at Bridger as he was brought back into the dock but I wasn't surprised when he fixed his gaze on the floor. His lip was quivering slightly and I hoped it was a sign of how scared he was.

Before Mr Justice Griffith-Williams made his decision on the sentence Bridger would be given, both barristers had one final chance to speak. Elwen had asked if she could read out a victim impact statement from Coral. This was a longer statement to the one my wife would soon read out on the court steps. She and Hayley had spent many hours working on it, as they wanted to convey to the judge how much our lives had been destroyed by the actions of this disgusting man.

"'I am Coral Joyce Jones and I am the mother of April Sue-Lyn Jones,'" Elwen began, as a hush descended on the room.

The mood was very strange. Everyone's relief at the verdict was palpable but there was hardly a party atmosphere. April was never far from anyone's thoughts and, with every sentence that was spoken, came a reminder that we'd all been brought together as the result of the most unimaginable tragedy.

Elwen continued to read: "'In addition to previous statements I have made I also wish to make a statement in relation to the devastating effect the loss of our beautiful daughter April has had on me and my family.'"

Coral inhaled sharply but she was much stronger than I'd expected. As ever, I took her hand in mine and we both stared straight at the man who'd shattered our existence into a million pieces. We could only hope that soon he'd understand a little of the pain we felt every day, a pain that would never ease with the passing of time.

"'Words alone cannot describe how we are feeling or how we manage to function on a daily basis,'" Elwen went on. "'I would never ever want any other family to go through what we are and will go through for the rest of our lives.'"

She then read the words Coral had lovingly written about April's childhood and about our lives before this horrific ordeal began. For the first time that day, I felt a lump spring to my throat, but I managed to hold it together. So much of the trial had focused on April's brutal death. It was almost as if her short life had been momentarily forgotten but now people were finally getting the chance to hear what a wonderful little girl she had been.

"'April was born prematurely, weighing only 4lb 2oz, and was in intensive care for two weeks,'" Elwen said. "'She has always been a little fighter and we later found out that she had a hole in her heart.'"

"'When she was around three years old we noticed she was becoming clumsy, so after numerous visits to the doctors they finally diagnosed April with cerebral palsy down her left side from her hip to her leg.'"

"'She became a guinea pig for other children in that she was measured for a special suit to support her growing bones, and if this suit was successful they would make suits for other children.'"

"'We would have to massage her legs and get her to do exercises because she would have pain in her legs constantly. She very rarely moaned about the pain and would be always on the go, wanting to go out to play with her friends.'"

"'April ruled our lives. She was the youngest and, because of her various disabilities, we would have to provide some kind of care for her all the time.'"

"'Paul would get her ready for school and then I would be there when she came home. I still cannot go into her bedroom to sort out her clothes because the pain of her not being there is indescribable."

"'I have to watch Jazmin and Harley grieve for the loss of their little sister, whom they would sometimes carry upstairs because she was in too much pain to walk."

"'I have to see people whom I have known for years cross the road to avoid me because they do not know what to say to me. At Christmas I tried to make it as normal as possible but would find myself breaking down in tears when I would be in a shop and would see April's favourite Hello Kitty things and anything pink, which was her favourite colour."

"'I broke my heart writing Christmas cards, wondering whether I should put April's name on them. In the end I decided to just put a pink bow instead of April's name as a symbol of hope for our lovely girl.'"

A few people in the public gallery had begun to dab their eyes. Even some of the jurors were crying. Elwen paused a little, before continuing: "'I will never forget the night of the first of October 2012."

"'This was the night that we allowed our daughter April to go out to play with her friends, something she has done hundreds of times before, and this is the night that she never came home. Since that night, the estate is quiet, as the children are no longer allowed to go out to play as they used to."

"'As April's mother I will live with the guilt of letting her go out to play on the estate that night for the rest of my life. She fought to come into the world, she fought to stay in this world, and he has taken her not only from us, but from everyone who loved her."

"'I will never see her smile again or hear her stomping around upstairs and on the landing. We will never see her bring home her first boyfriend and Paul will never walk her down the aisle. How will we ever get over it?'"

I bowed my head for a few seconds. Words could never express how the loss of April had affected us, but Coral's statement came close.

Brendan Kelly then rose to speak for Bridger but there wasn't much any lawyer could do for him now.

'It is likely he will spend the rest of his life in custody,' his barrister admitted. 'I'm loath to raise this but the only mitigation is that he is not a repeat offender.'

At this point, I caught sight of Bridger nodding his head. He was truly deluded – acting as if the fact he had never murdered a child before entitled him to some kind of special treatment.

But, finally, Mr Justice Griffith-Williams turned to him in the dock. This was the moment we'd all been waiting for.

'The sentence for murder is life imprisonment but I have to decide the length of the minimum term you must serve,' he began, gravely.

'Schedule 21 of the Criminal Justice Act 2003 provides that if the court considers the seriousness of the offence is exceptionally high, the appropriate starting point should be a whole life order.

'The cases which would normally fall within that category include the murder of a child which involves the abduction of the child or sexual or sadistic motivation.

'While I am satisfied that the seriousness of your offending is exceptionally high, I must nonetheless consider whether a substantial minimum term, in excess of a starting point of thirty years, would be sufficient to reflect the gravity of these offences.'

The courtroom was eerily silent as everyone hung on his every word.

'For the last four weeks, the court has listened to compelling evidence of your guilt, evidence which has also demonstrated that you are a pathological and glib liar,' the judge continued.

'There is no doubt in my mind that you are a paedophile who has for some time harboured sexual and morbid fantasies about young girls, storing on your laptop not only images of pre-pubescent and pubescent girls, but foul pornography of the gross sexual abuse of young children.

'What prompted you on Monday, the first of October, to live out one of those fantasies is a matter for speculation but it may have been the combination of the ending of one sexual relationship and your drinking.

'Whatever, you set out to find a little girl to abuse. I am not sure you targeted April specifically – it was probably fortuitous that she can be seen on some of the images you stored on your laptop of her older sister – but you were on the prowl for a young girl.

'April would not have been afraid of you partly because you have some charm. She may well have seen you about the estate and you let her know your son was a friend of her brother, Harley – just as you had tried to charm her sister, Jazmin, into allowing you to be her Facebook friend by mentioning your links to her parents.'

I instinctively reached for Jazmin's hand and took it in mine. Yet again, she'd shown maturity and composure beyond her years and was sitting in dignified silence.

The judge went on: 'And so it was, that innocently and trustingly, April got into your Land Rover smiling and happy. What followed is known only to you but this much is certain – you abducted her for a sexual purpose and then murdered her and disposed of her body to hide the evidence of your sexual abuse of her, which probably occurred on the way from the estate to your home because there is some sixty minutes of your time which cannot be accounted for.

'I cannot infer from the evidence where you murdered her but if she was alive when you took her to the house, she died there. How you disposed of her body must remain a mystery. It will serve no purpose for me to speculate as to what happened but all the indications are that you burnt at least a part of her in the wood burner.

'The grief of April's parents cannot be overstated. They lived with the torment of a missing daughter, praying that she would be found alive and then, following your arrest, with the knowledge that you were providing the police with no assistance at all as to her whereabouts.

'To add to that torment, they have had to endure the spectacle of your hypocritical sympathy for their loss and of your tears, flowing not because of any regret for your crimes, but because of your enduring self-pity.

'Without the knowledge of what happened to April, her parents will probably never come to terms with their grievous loss, described so eloquently in the impact statement. It is to be hoped, for their sakes, for the sakes of Jazmin and Harley and for the sakes of all those who mourn April, that the verdicts will bring some measure of closure.

'Your offences were aggravated by their premeditation and by the destruction of at least a part of her body and the concealment of the rest. It is also a relevant consideration that you not only abducted April with a sexual motive but then sexually abused her in some way.

'While I have had regard to the absence of any relevant conviction, I have no doubt there can be only one sentence.

'For the offence of murder, I sentence you to life imprisonment with a whole life order. There will be no separate penalties on counts one and three.'

Bridger simply closed his eyes and bowed his head before he was taken down to the cells for the final time.

Around half an hour passed before we were taken to the court steps to face the press. Just like when the verdict was announced, it took a few minutes for Coral and me to get our heads around what had happened. As the people surrounding us hugged and cried, we were simply overwhelmed with relief that Bridger would never be allowed to walk the streets again.

In the midst of the flurry of activity, we managed to say our goodbyes to the court staff and volunteers. As we thanked them for their kindness, many of them were in tears.

I took Coral's arm as we walked out to the front of the court, with Dave and Hayley following closely behind us. I was glad I wasn't the one who had to do the talking. Coral was shaking but she had a determined look in her eyes.

*

Coral recalls:

My legs had all but turned to jelly as Paul and I walked out to the court steps. The police had put up a barrier between us and the reporters, but it didn't stop me feeling panicked. I remembered the last time I'd spoken directly to the press, just two days after April was taken, when I appealed for information on her whereabouts – and a knot of dread formed in my stomach.

'Don't worry,' said Rhian. 'They won't be able to get any closer to you than this.'

'Thanks,' I replied, weakly, remembering how terrified I'd been as I'd sat in front of them on that awful day seven months previously.

Andy John was already standing by the microphone, as he was due to speak first. With Dave and Hayley on either side of us, Paul put his arm around me as Andy began to talk.

'A short while ago, the jury in this case concluded that the defendant, Mark Bridger, was guilty of all offences charged,' Andy said. 'The strength of evidence was overwhelming and he was responsible for the most horrific of crimes – the abduction and murder of a vulnerable five-year-old child, April Jones.

'Justice has been done and Mark Bridger, an evil and manipulative individual, will have his liberty taken away from him for the rest of his life. He abducted and murdered April and has then gone to enormous lengths to destroy evidence, conceal his involvement and avoid detection.

'It is as a consequence of an intense and thorough investigation, using the best possible resources, experts and prosecution team, that the evidence gathered has proved that he, and he alone, was responsible for these horrific crimes.

'April's parents, Coral and Paul, and their family have shown such enormous strength, courage and dignity during the most difficult of times. Neither I nor the majority of the public can ever begin to imagine what this family has gone through and continues to go through.'

Now, it was my turn. I took a deep breath and started to read out the statement I'd prepared just a few hours earlier.

'We are relieved that Mark Bridger has today been found guilty of the murder of our beautiful daughter April,' I began.

I was vaguely aware of one reporter asking me to get closer to the microphone, so I stepped forward. I felt light-headed with adrenaline and prayed I wouldn't collapse.

'April will be forever in our hearts and we are so moved by the overwhelming support we have had from so many people all over the world,' I continued. My voice was much stronger than I thought it would be and I was glad it didn't betray how jittery I was inside. Strangely I didn't feel like crying. I was still a little numb and I knew it would take a while to come to terms with what we'd just been through.

'Paul and I would like to thank Dyfed-Powys Police for the support they have given us, the investigation team, the search teams from all over the UK, and our family liaison officers.

'We would like to thank our family and friends and the community of Machynlleth. Without their support, we do not know how we would have got through the last seven months since April was so cruelly taken from us.

'We would like to thank the media for the respectful way in which they have reported April's story, and we would like to take time now to be with our family and to try and come to terms with the loss of April.'

Paul again wrapped his arm around me as I finished reading. It was perfect timing, as I was sure my legs were ready to buckle beneath me. When I see footage of that day, I'm amazed at how calm I look. At the time, I was convinced I was visibly shaking with a strange mix of grief and relief. The verdict would never bring April back, nor would it give our family closure. But at least we were safe in the knowledge that Bridger could never put anyone else through the hell we were forced to live, day after day.

Ed Beltrami, chief crown prosecutor for Wales, spoke last.

'We welcome today's verdict, which brings to a close a difficult and challenging criminal process,' he said. 'Ever since his first interview with police in October last year, Mark Bridger has relentlessly spun a web of lies and half-truths in order to try and distance himself from the truly horrific nature of the crime he perpetrated.

'He has refused to take responsibility for what he did to April and has stopped at nothing to try and cover his tracks. Despite his best efforts to evade justice, he has been brought to account by a highly professional investigation by Dyfed-Powys Police, which was acknowledged by the trial judge today, coupled with the diligence and hard work of the prosecution team.

'Working together, we have been able to comprehensively dismantle Bridger's version of events and expose him as a violent, cold-hearted murderer and a calculated liar. I would like to record our thanks to everyone who supported the prosecution of this case, particularly the child witnesses.

'One girl in particular, aged only seven, gave vital evidence in the case regarding the abduction and her parents should be very proud of her.'

I thought of Amy and the testimony she'd given and how grateful Paul and I would always be to her. I dreaded to think what might have happened had she not been so brave and honest.

'At the very heart of this case are April's family, who have been through – and continue to go through – an ordeal of appalling magnitude,' Ed Beltrami went on. 'They have conducted themselves with a humbling dignity throughout.

'We can only hope – and I'm sure I speak for all of the prosecution team – that today's verdict will be of some help to them as they continue to try and come to terms with their terrible loss.'

A little while after the press conference, Dave and Hayley dropped us off at our cottage for the final time. The next day, we'd be going home to Machynlleth, where we'd have to attempt to get on with the rest of our lives.

It was strange saying goodbye to them. For the best part of a year, we'd seen them almost every day, but now the trial was over their visits and calls would be scaled back. Although they'd still be our FLOs, they would have far fewer official duties. We understood that they had to be deployed elsewhere, but it was still a wrench.

'Give us a call if you need anything,' Dave said, with a smile. Coral and I both knew then that we'd always be able to rely on them, long after April's name had disappeared from the front pages of the newspapers, which gave us a crumb of comfort.

When we got back to the cottage, Ryan Parry and Emma Foster, two reporters from the *Sun* newspaper, visited. After much deliberation, we'd decided to give them the first post-trial interview, which was to be run over the next three days in the newspaper. We'd already had a few chats with them and we felt we could trust them with our story. We knew the interview would be hard but we were desperate to make sure April was remembered not just as the victim of the most brutal of crimes, but as the daughter we knew and loved – our darling little girl with her gorgeous, big, brown eyes and huge heart.

The previous weekend, Ryan and Emma had visited us in Machynlleth and a photographer had taken pictures of our house and April's bedroom. Both Coral and I had found this very hard and even the photographer had been in tears when he saw April's teddies stretched across her empty bed. The *Sun* had offered to pay us for the story and, at one point, I'd found myself crying, wondering if we'd sold April out. But after many emotional conversations Coral and I decided to accept the newspaper's offer of a financial reward. Not only did we want to tell our side of the story after being silent for so long, we also had to think of our family's future. With neither of us able to work, we'd spent many a sleepless night wondering how we'd support Jazmin and Harley as they grew older.

As Jazmin was studying media at college, the newspaper had also offered her an internship in exchange for our cooperation. These opportunities are obviously few and far between, and we knew how good a work placement with the biggest newspaper in the country would look on Jazmin's CV. All things considered, we felt we couldn't turn the offer down, but it didn't make things any easier.

We'd handed over treasured family photographs of April. There were pictures of her as a tiny baby, covered in wires in her incubator and being bathed in the mixing bowl, and others from when she was a little older, at birthday parties and on days out.

'She was our little princess,' Coral had sobbed to Ryan and Emma, as they'd looked through them. Despite her pain, she'd managed to speak articulately and movingly about our daughter. 'She was always smiling and laughing and so full of life. Even though she had cerebral palsy and other health problems, she didn't let it stop her. She was our little fighter from the beginning.

'No one can ever replace her. Even though she was a tiny little thing, she had a huge presence. Our lives will never be the same without her. Her death has shattered our entire family.'

'Today has pulled me apart,' I wrote in my diary that evening. 'I cried from start to finish. It hurts so deeply. My pain at having lost April doesn't lessen with time. Things just seem to get tougher and, in moments like this, I'm so tired and so, so sad. I try to do the best for my family but I wonder if I've done the wrong thing. I miss my April. She was my dream little daughter.'

On the day of the verdict, the process was a lot less formal than the statements we'd given on the court steps, and Ryan and Emma made us feel at ease. While we'd touched on April's childhood and the day she'd been taken from us in our previous conversations, they now wanted to hear all about our reaction to the verdict and the sentencing. Neither of us was in the mood to hold back.

'Bridger is just a monster,' I told them. 'He was prepared to do or say anything to wriggle out of what he's done. He has done such an awful thing and yet he couldn't own up, even with all the evidence stacked against him.

'He honestly thought it was worth the risk; that he could get away with it. It was just a sexual fantasy for him at the end of the day, and our April paid for it with her life.'

'He's put a hole in our heart,' Coral added. 'He ripped a happy family apart. He's evil.'

They asked us how we'd feel if we were ever to come into contact with Bridger again. I wasn't sure how to respond. I could feel the anger that had been bubbling inside me for eight long months coming to the surface.

'Bridger has never had one thought for our family or what we've been going through,' I found myself saying. 'He's just a coward, an evil coward.

'If I was ever put face-to-face with him I don't think I could bring myself to talk to him. I'm pretty sure I'd just strangle him.

'He picked on a five-year-old little girl who had health problems and couldn't defend herself against him. How could anyone do that?'

Coral was in tears so I put my arm around her and tried to console her. 'He's taken everything,' she wept. 'He's taken my little girl from me, he's destroyed our family in one go.

'And he hasn't just wrecked our lives; he's wrecked the lives of our other children. Our friends, our neighbours have all been hurt by this. It has hurt loads of people.'

Of course, April's body still hadn't been recovered, and Ryan and Emma wanted to ask us if we had any hope of finding the rest of her remains. After the verdict had been announced, it had emerged that Bridger had confessed to a Catholic priest called Father Barry O'Sullivan that he'd dumped our little girl in the River Dovey. Father O'Sullivan had been asked by the prison to counsel Bridger but had been left so traumatised by their conversations that he'd needed therapy himself. However, on account of the forensic evidence, Bridger's claim had been largely dismissed by the police, who were still convinced he'd cut up her little body and scattered the remains.

'Lots of people have questioned him, but he's refused to tell us all along where her body is,' Coral said. 'If he's lied to police, barristers and the judge, there's no way he'll tell me where my little girl is. Now he's been found guilty he could tell us, but he hasn't.'

After the interview was finished, we posed for pictures and recorded a video for the newspaper's website. When Ryan and Emma left, we packed up our things before going for a pub meal with my mum, Dai, Fil and Jazz. We had just finished our dinner when one of the customers in the pub noticed us and came over to shake our hands.

'Mr and Mr Jones,' he said. 'I was so pleased for you today. Let me buy you a drink.'

'That's very kind of you,' I replied. This man was amiable without being overbearing, like some of the people who cornered us in the street. It was still strange to be recognised but nice to know the public were behind us.

Jazmin, Fil and I played some table tennis and pool while my mum, Dai and Coral went back to the house. Coral was exhausted and needed an early night. When we got back to the cottage around 10 p.m., I felt drained. I went to write in my diary and the tears started to flow. The conviction was like a massive weight being lifted off my shoulders but there was still a huge hole in our lives.

'It's been a long, hard but good day,' I wrote. 'Coral spoke so well and so clearly. I've never been so proud of a woman in all my life.

'The law has sentenced Mark Bridger to the maximum. We couldn't ask for any more but in a way we're still disappointed with the end result. I don't think he'll ever suffer like we have, but it's good to know he's away for the rest of his life. I'm glad to get it over with but now I just have a numb feeling. Coral and I will just have to rest now and take stock of our situation and think about what to do next.

'We just can't thank everyone enough for all their help: Dyfed-Powys Police (what a team), the search teams, the locals in Mach, the CPS, the jury and the judge, friends, family and our country for their support. We thank them all from the bottom of our hearts.

'I love you, April Jones – we all love and miss you. Dad xxx.'

11

The Aftermath

I thought I'd sleep like a log on the night after the verdict, but I was actually pretty restless. Coral didn't get much rest either and we both got up early. There were so many thoughts running through our heads that it was hard to switch off. Above all, we both wondered how we'd readjust to normal life now the trial was over. For eight months our sole purpose had been to get justice for April. Now we had achieved that, all we were left with was our overpowering grief.

It was a beautiful morning, so we had breakfast outside our little cottage before packing our things into Dai's van. On the way home, I noticed that the newspaper billboards outside every newsagent and convenience store bore April's name. Even though we'd been in the media spotlight for almost a year, it was still strange seeing our daughter's name plastered everywhere and our

189

faces on the front pages of the newspapers. Thankfully, the *Sun* article was sensitively written and we were both happy with the end result.

We got back to Machynlleth by mid-afternoon. Harley was away for the weekend with a friend's family and Jazmin had gone out for a few hours with my mum and Dai, so the house was deathly quiet. Both Coral and I were fighting back tears as we stepped over the threshold and the dogs ran to greet us.

The lack of sleep had begun to catch up with Coral, so she went for a nap while I walked the dogs along the riverside. Enjoying the sunlight on my face, it felt good to be outdoors again. It hadn't felt natural to me being cooped up inside all day.

As ever, my thoughts turned to April. The next thing Coral and I would have to consider was our little girl's funeral, but we didn't know when her remains would be released to us. Even when they were, all we'd have would be a few tiny bone fragments. Coral had told the *Sun* that she feared going to her grave without knowing where April was, just like Winnie Johnson, the mother of the Moors Murder victim Keith Bennett. I'd begun to accept that this was a strong possibility.

Coral and I had also begun to discuss the idea of a campaign against child pornography. Although we'd been warned about the indecent images before the court case, we'd had no idea of the extent of Bridger's vile obsession until we'd attended the trial. Quite frankly we were horrified at how readily available such depraved material was online. We were left in no doubt that the disgusting content Bridger had accessed in the lead-up to April's abduction had fuelled his sick fantasies.

We were bemused that his online activity hadn't been picked

up before April was taken, as he'd viewed so many illegal pictures, but not as bemused as we were about the fact he'd managed to access these images in the first place. We had no idea why the major search engines, such as Google and Bing, which was owned by Microsoft, didn't have proper safeguards in place to automatically filter such disgusting content, to ensure it didn't appear in search results.

We didn't buy the idea that they weren't capable of this – these were some of the biggest corporations in the world, with billions of pounds and scores of experts at their disposal. If they didn't clean up their act, Coral and I believed we needed to get tough with them and hit them where it really hurt – in the pocket. We saw no reason why the law couldn't be changed to ensure they'd be liable for huge fines if they didn't do enough to stop paedophiles successfully searching for illegal images.

We weren't naive; we knew that ridding the internet of child pornography wouldn't be enough to stamp out paedophilia completely, but we hoped it could go some way to addressing the problem. We mentioned this to Ryan and Emma from the *Sun* and they agreed to help arrange a meeting with Dr Sara Payne, a high-profile campaigner against child abuse who wrote a regular column for the newspaper.

Like most parents, we were horrified when Sara's eight-year-old daughter Sarah was abducted in the summer of 2000, while she played near her grandparents' house in Kingston Gorse, West Sussex. Sarah and her brother Lee had been playing hide and seek but, after a short while, Sarah fell over and hurt herself. She decided she wanted to go back to see her grandmother, Les, who had stayed at home, as she was tired after cooking a large family meal. Lee tried to run after her and had only taken his eyes off her for a second when she disappeared.

After seventeen tortuous days, Sarah's little body was found in a field around fifteen miles from where she was last seen alive. The story was on the front page of newspapers for weeks and was the leading item on all the television news bulletins. I'd just moved in with Coral and, along with the rest of the nation, we watched in horror, unable to imagine the agony of this poor girl's family. We never dreamed that one day we'd understand their pain more than anyone ever should.

Following a large-scale police investigation, a paedophile called Roy Whiting was charged and later convicted of Sarah's murder. In an excruciating twist, it transpired that Sarah's brother Lee had seen Whiting waiting in a white van yards from the beach just moments after he'd lost sight of his sister. Whiting had grinned at Lee, who had no idea that Sarah was inside, then waved as he drove off to abuse and kill her.

After the trial, it emerged that Whiting had been sentenced to four years in prison for sexually assaulting another eight-year-old girl five years previously. Shortly after he arrived in jail in 1995, he was assessed by a psychiatrist, who deemed him likely to reoffend. Despite the fact Whiting refused to attend a sex offenders' rehabilitation course, he was released after serving just over half of his sentence – meaning he was free to abduct and murder Sarah.

When Sara discovered this, she was naturally distraught and decided she had to act. With the help of the now-defunct tabloid newspaper, the *News of the World*, she began to campaign for a law that would give parents and guardians controlled access to the Sex

Offenders' Register. At the discretion of the relevant authorities, this would allow adults involved in the care of a young person to check whether individuals who came into contact with the child had any record of sexually abusing young people. This was partly modelled on the Crimes Against Children and Sexually Violent Offender Registration Act in the USA, more commonly known as Megan's Law. It was informally named after a seven-year-old girl, Megan Kanka, who was raped and murdered in 1994 by a neighbour with previous convictions for sexually assaulting children.

In 2011, after a decade-long fight, Sarah's Law – known officially as the Child Sex Offender Disclosure scheme – was finally introduced in the UK, by which point Sara had become one of the most respected campaigners in the country. She was awarded an MBE for her work in 2008, which was followed by an honorary doctorate from the Open University in 2012. She has also served as an adviser to the UK government.

When we met Sara in London on 4 June, Sarah's Law had already helped concerned adults identify hundreds of convicted paedophiles who had access to children close to them. Sara had been absolutely unwavering in her determination to have the law changed, and we knew her advice would be very useful if we wanted to drive through our own changes.

Ryan and Emma arrived in Machynlleth in the early afternoon of the Monday following the trial. They had asked us if we'd like to bring Jazmin and Harley to London with us and we agreed this would be a good idea. We'd spent so much time apart from them over the last month that we decided it would be nice to do something as a family. We also thought the change of scenery would benefit us all.

Jazmin and I travelled with Ryan in one car, while Coral and Harley went with Emma in another. The journey took over four hours and this gave both Coral and me a chance to speak to the reporters about the campaign. We arrived at our hotel around 6.30 p.m. and, shortly afterwards, we were taken out for a meal.

Over the course of various discussions throughout the day, Coral and I had told Ryan and Emma that we'd like to start a petition against the child pornography that seemed so readily available on the internet. The *Sun* quickly agreed to give us its backing and we agreed on a few key objectives.

There was one thing on which we were absolutely clear: we wanted it to be made illegal for search engines to return links to content which depicted any kind of child sex abuse, and we wanted the companies involved to be liable for substantial fines if they didn't comply with the legislation we proposed. Very quickly, we began to refer to this as April's Law.

We decided that we also wanted to make it compulsory for internet companies to help fund policing of the web, and we wanted the government to dedicate greater financial resources to clamping down on illegal images of children online.

In our view, the combined funds would allow them to employ technical experts to identify abusive images and people searching for child pornography. We also wanted on-screen warnings for people who viewed this content, to make browsers aware of the nature of such websites before they entered them. Coral suggested that if a person was caught trying to access the same illegal website on a second occasion, the police should be notified immediately and an investigation launched.

We met Sara in a coffee shop across from our hotel early the next morning. I was slightly surprised to discover she was on crutches. She greeted us warmly and was very open about her health problems, telling us she'd been paralysed down her left side after suffering a stroke several years previously. As we sat down and ordered drinks, we learned just how much she had been through since Sarah's death. Sara and Mike had been childhood sweethearts but the grief of losing their much-loved daughter had torn their marriage apart. However, while they were in the process of separating, Sara discovered she was pregnant with their fifth child, Ellie, who was now nine. Despite all of the obstacles she'd faced, Sara had flatly refused to give up and remained wholeheartedly committed to campaigning against the sexual abuse of children. This only cemented our admiration for her.

When the conversation turned to the campaign, however, I took a bit of a back seat. It was important for Coral to talk to Sara as much as she could, mother to mother.

Coral recalls:
Although Sara immediately struck me as friendly and sympathetic, my overriding memory of her is of her fire. I was in awe of her determination and resilience. We immediately felt her presence when we walked into the room. It was clear she was no softly spoken shrinking violet. Life had dealt her so many cruel blows, but every time she had come back fighting.

When she began to tell me about the first, dreadful months after Sarah was taken, I saw so much of myself in her. Like me, she'd been a normal mum from a humble background. She'd never craved the limelight, or the finer things in life. She and Mike didn't have a big, fancy house or a flashy car in the driveway. What they did have was the love of their beautiful children, whom they would have laid down their lives for – and they wouldn't have had it any other way.

But, like me, Sara's world was turned upside down in the blink of an eye when she made what seems like the most mundane of decisions – allowing her daughter to play outside.

Another *Sun* reporter, Antonella Lazzeri, had been sent to cover the meeting but I almost forgot my words were being recorded as I spoke candidly to Sara.

'Does the pain ever go away?' I asked. My hands had started to shake and I could barely hold my coffee cup.

Sara put a supportive hand on my arm. 'No,' she replied. 'I'd like to tell you it does, but it really doesn't. It does lessen with time and you get a lot more good days than bad.'

I told Sara all about the months before the trial: how I was often unable to get out of bed and how, some days, I'd survive on a few tiny mouthfuls of Ready Brek. She nodded sympathetically; she too had been barely able to function in the aftermath of Sarah's death. She and Mike had frequently rowed, as she'd spend hours staring mindlessly at the television while he was at work, barely attempting to do the chores or cook dinner for the children. She'd pull herself together to give newspaper interviews or make television appearances to speak about Sarah's Law, but privately her life was in disarray.

We then began to talk about the campaign. I asked her a bit about Sarah's Law, before we moved on to talking about child pornography. It still made my stomach lurch to think of the images I'd seen in court, but I knew I had to do it for April.

'Paul and I would love to work with you,' I told her. 'There's no reason for these sites to be there. If you're looking at a paedophile site, there has to be something wrong with you.'

Sara nodded in agreement.

'I didn't want to look at those pictures in court, but I had to,' I said. 'They were just horrible. Why should they be on the internet?'

Sara squeezed my hand, shaking her head in disgust. 'I know, Coral,' she replied.

'I believe in a warning flashing up when you go looking for those sites,' I went on. 'One time, you might have made a mistake, but a second? You should be warned and reported to the police. If that had happened to Mark Bridger, it might have stopped him. This campaign will give me something to focus on. I fear if I stop, I'll crack.'

'You won't,' Sara replied, firmly. 'You're stronger than you think.'

We then had some photographs taken, before we recorded a video for the Sun's website. Being filmed was a curious experience, as chatting to Sara was as natural as talking to an old friend. Speaking about the campaign, I felt animated and passionate, but when we moved on to April, tears sprang to my eyes.

'I was the one who said she could go out,' I said, taking a deep breath. 'So I feel guilty.'

'But every child should have that right,' Sara replied. 'Every child has the right to play, to go on their bikes. Surely that's what childhood is about?'

I sighed and nodded. It was all just so cruel. Since April had been taken, I'd been tempted to wrap Harley and Jazmin in cotton wool and never let them out of my sight. But I knew this wasn't healthy or normal and that I had to let them develop into young adults without constant scrutiny.

Soon the camera stopped rolling and it was time to say our goodbyes. Sara said she'd like to keep in touch.

'Coral, you didn't do anything wrong that day,' she told me. 'You wanted to give your daughter a treat because she'd done well at school. Why shouldn't she have had a treat?'

'I said it was OK, as long as it was just for a little while,' I replied. 'I just thought, I'll give her fifteen minutes extra. It wasn't even dark.'

'I drove myself mad with the "if onlys",' Sara admitted. 'But you can't keep beating yourself up. What could you have done, locked her in her bedroom? You can't keep blaming yourself. It will kill you.'

I couldn't quite bring myself to accept that I'd ever get over the guilt I felt for letting April out that night, but I was grateful to Sara for trying her best to convince me I hadn't been in the wrong.

She then gave me a big hug and handed me a piece of paper with her mobile number on it. I knew we wouldn't have the time to speak as regularly as we'd like – we were both busy mums with families to attend to – but it was comforting to know she was at the other end of the phone whenever I needed a chat.

Coral seemed buoyed by the meeting with Sara. As we made our way back to the hotel, I could almost sense some of her old vibrancy returning.

'Hopefully we can make some changes,' she said. 'The internet definitely had a lot to do with April's death.'

'I know,' I said, sadly, wondering for what seemed like the hundredth time if Bridger's desire to abuse children would have got so out of hand if he hadn't had access to such horrible websites.

'If I can save just one more child, I'll be happy,' she went on. 'This is for all families, Paul. Not just for us.'

'I'm really proud of you for doing this,' I told her. 'Let's hope we can make a difference.'

To take our mind off things, the *Sun* had arranged a trip that afternoon for us and the children to go on the London Eye. We all enjoyed the experience and Coral and I were even treated to champagne. We were then whisked off to an Italian restaurant for dinner, where we had a lovely meal.

As we ate, I felt like I was being torn in two different directions. It was so nice be able to treat Harley and Jazmin after everything they'd been through, and we'd never have been able to afford such a lavish day out in London if we'd had to pay for it ourselves. But, on the other hand, we were under no illusions that none of us would have been sitting there if we hadn't lost April. London was exciting, but it was also busy and bustling and a little bit out of our comfort zone. Coral and I would have happily never taken another trip or had another meal out again if it could have brought April back to us.

We got back to the hotel around 8 p.m. and I wrote in my diary while Coral, Jazmin and Harley watched a bit of television.

'Today has been a good day,' I wrote. 'I can see a difference in Coral. With something to fight for, she's more herself. I hope this will make her stronger and help her on the road to recovery.

'Coral and Sara got on very well. They talked about their suffering and how between them they could maybe get some of these pornographic sites taken down. Both of them felt this would make a serious difference, as surely these sites can only fuel sexual predators.

'As for me, I struggle for a cause, but perhaps just being there for Coral, Jazz and Harley is enough. Hopefully this will help me on my road to recovery. It's nice to be able to spoil the kids but I feel very tired and tearful when we're out together, enjoying ourselves without April. It still makes me feel sad and low.

'I love you, April. Dad xxx.'

The next morning, we were woken by our alarms at 6.30 a.m. We'd agreed to do our first proper television interview since the trial, with the ITV programme *This Morning*. We had a quick breakfast before the taxi picked us up at 8 a.m. and we travelled to the studios.

Coral and I would be interviewed by presenters Phillip Schofield and Holly Willoughby, where we would have the chance to speak about our campaign and how we hoped to change the law in April's name. Phillip Schofield in particular had taken an interest in April's case from the very start, appealing for information on Twitter just the day after she vanished, so we hoped he'd be sympathetic to our plight. Emma, Jazmin and Harley came along too. They were allowed to watch our interview from behind the camera.

Phillip and Holly are national icons and we wondered what they would be like off camera. Rumours often abound about how well-known celebrities can be demanding and dismissive in real life, when faced with the prospect of interacting with the general public. This certainly wasn't true of Phillip and Holly. They couldn't have been kinder to us and truly lived up to their reputations. They spent a few minutes coaching us on the interview before we went on air and telling us how they would prompt us when they wanted us to speak.

Appearing on a show like *This Morning* is very different to watching it at home, where everything looks so effortless and natural. In reality, it can only be described as organised chaos. As well as Phillip and Holly onscreen, there were some thirty people buzzing around in the background, running around with clipboards and cameras or doing make-up. The team was obviously very talented and we were in awe of how they managed to make the programme look so slick as it was being broadcast.

We were told we'd probably be on air for around six minutes but, in the end, the interview lasted twice as long. We barely noticed – we had so much to say on April and the campaign that we weren't sure how it could have been cut down.

'These indecent images should be removed,' I said, when we were asked about child pornography on the internet.

'I'd like to do something in April's name,' Coral agreed. 'If I can save just one person, it's better than none.'

Afterwards, Phillip and Holly chatted to the children and signed some autographs for them. I also got a signed photograph of Holly for one of my friends, who was a big fan of hers. Needless to say, he was delighted.

In the afternoon, Coral and Jazmin went to have their hair done, while Harley and I did a bit of clothes shopping. We had a nice late lunch with Ryan and Emma, before we said goodbye to them and caught a taxi to Euston Station to begin the long train journey back to Machynlleth.

On the way home, Coral had a chance to catch up with her emails and Facebook messages and, already, lots of people had contacted her to say they wanted to support our campaign. But, as we knew all too well, a few good days are almost always followed by several bad ones. We got home around 9 p.m. that evening after catching our connection at Birmingham and Coral was so drained she went straight to bed. I took the dogs for a short walk and I found myself crying.

'Now I'm home, a sadness comes over me,' I wrote in my diary when I got back in. 'I look around and, knowing there's no April, I find so many things that trigger me. It all comes back to me and I feel so sad and down. It's an awful feeling, so hard to explain.

'I wish I could see your face and hear your voice, April. I find it impossible to believe I'll never hear or see you again. I miss you and it's so tough and unfair. I find myself thinking of you a lot. I don't cry as much but I still feel low. I have to carry on but at forty-four years old, I shouldn't be living my life without you.

'I love you, April Sue-Lyn Jones.

'Your very sad and sorry Dad xxx.'

On the Friday of our first week back at home, Dave popped round for a visit. It was the longest we'd gone without seeing him since April was taken. We'd only spent a week apart from our FLOs, but it was like walking without our crutches. We were so used to them pointing us in the right direction and explaining everything.

Nonetheless, it was great to see Dave and to catch up. He

stayed for over an hour and we told him about our week over a cup of tea.

On the Saturday, we did an interview with *Woman's Own* magazine, which seemed to go OK. Coral had a chat on the phone with one of the writers in London before they sent a photographer to do some pictures. He suggested we go to Borth beach on the Ceredigion coast, as we'd often taken April there after school if the weather was nice. It was only a half-hour car journey and we agreed, as he promised it wouldn't take long. However, we were starting to discover that photoshoots often had the habit of overrunning and we spent several hours posing on the sand. This wiped Coral out, so she went to bed as soon as we got home around 5 p.m.

I didn't feel like resting, so I took Autumn and Storm down to the river, where I collected some stones for the memorial we'd been slowly building for April on the communal green area outside our home. We'd decided to call it April's Garden, or *Gardd April* in Welsh. Lots of the neighbours had helped and it now looked beautiful.

Of course, almost everything we were given for the garden was in April's favourite colour. There were pink bows, pink soft toys and even a pink doll's house. Someone had built us a bench and a local business had donated garden furniture. Children had played happily on Bryn-y-Gog for decades before April was taken but in the months since her disappearance many parents had, understandably, been reluctant to let their kids out of their sight, even for a few minutes. We hoped that April's Garden would be a symbol of hope, reminding them that the children had a right to play on the estate without fear.

The garden had been attracting a lot of visitors from outside the town. On that day, a lady from Welshpool, a town that lay forty miles away on the English border, had brought her daughter to the garden to lay a teddy in memory of April. The little girl was five years old and she bore an uncanny resemblance to my daughter. She had the same mousy brown hair, slight frame and impish smile. It almost stopped me in my tracks.

'She's very like April, isn't she?' I said to her mum.

'Many people have said that,' she replied.

We chatted for around twenty minutes and the girl's mum told me that they often visited Machynlleth, as they had a caravan nearby. She'd always found the locals so welcoming and had never for a second doubted that her little girl would be safe here. Naturally she was deeply distressed when she'd heard about April's abduction. It was a poignant moment and I had to bite my lip to stop myself from crying but it was lovely to see this little girl enjoying the garden in the sunshine.

I then took a walk up Penrach, where April and I had spent so many happy afternoons picking flowers and eating fruit. I'd been told that a few local women – we are still not sure of their identities – had erected their own memorial to our daughter on her favourite hill. They'd knitted lots of little pink squares and covered one of the trees in them. It had affectionately become known as the hugging tree.

I'd been putting off visiting the hugging tree, as walking up Penrach was very painful. Not only did it hold so many cherished memories of April, it was where I'd walked with Autumn and Storm on the morning of the day she disappeared, unaware of the nightmare that was about to unfold. However, both Coral and

I were deeply touched that people could take the time to fashion such an elaborate tribute to our little girl and I decided the time had come for me to see it for myself.

The hugging tree was near the summit of the hill, where I'd often carried April on my shoulders when her legs grew tired. I'd managed to hold back the tears as I chatted to the little girl from Welshpool and her mum but now I couldn't stop them as the tree slowly came into focus in a blaze of pink. All of the branches were adorned with intricately crafted squares of wool, each in different shades of my daughter's favourite colour. There were also Hello Kitty toys and ribbons, which she would have loved. Not a spot of the tree had been missed. I couldn't begin to imagine how much work had gone into making it look so lovely. It must have taken days, if not weeks, but these people had never drawn any attention to themselves, or asked for any thanks or recognition for their efforts. It was truly humbling.

I thought of April and how much she would have liked it. Now I was alone, I sobbed with abandon. As I looked down on Machynlleth and the white terraced houses of Bryn-y-Gog, I was crying so much I had to stop and catch my breath. I leaned against the hugging tree as the hot, salty tears streamed down my face. Even with Bridger locked away in jail, the agony would never truly be over.

I thought of the children who'd climb Penrach in the coming years, hand in hand with their parents. Perhaps they would sit at the top like April and I had, eating fruit and making up stories. I hoped the hugging tree would still be there to greet them – a symbol of love and hope in a town which in the eyes of the world was now overshadowed by evil and suffering.

As I walked down the hill and back into Machynlleth, I got upset again. The town looked so bare without the pink bows. When we had received the original letter saying that the council planned to remove them, the police had managed to persuade the councillors to leave them up until the end of the trial. But almost as soon as the verdict had been announced, they'd been taken down. Coral and I understood that Machynlleth had to move on and the town couldn't remain in a permanent state of mourning – but given how much April's disappearance had affected so many people, we felt that the councillors could have given us a few weeks' grace. The bows had been a symbol of hope for April and now it looked like she'd been forgotten. We knew that the vast majority of people in the town would have had no objection if the council had waited a little while before removing them. What hurt the most was that no one from the council seemed able to explain the decision to us personally. Coral played bingo with some of the councillors, yet they acted like nothing had happened.

'Give them an hour in my shoes and they'd feel differently,' she'd sobbed to me a few nights previously.

Eventually, we managed to come to a compromise and one large pink bow was allowed to remain by the town clock. In time, a metal bow will be galvanised in pink on the clock tower itself and a plaque will be erected in April's name. The bows provided such comfort to us during the most terrible time of our lives. We're glad they will never disappear completely from the town.

To add to our distress, I came home to find Coral in tears again. She'd received an anonymous letter which blamed us for April's disappearance. Her hands shaking, she handed it to me. My eye condition means I can only read with the aid of a special magnifying glass and it's generally a long, laboured process. But as I slowly picked over the words, I couldn't believe what I was reading.

'It's your own fault your daughter was taken,' it read. 'She should have been bathed and in her bed but she was out playing on the streets. It is disgusting. A little girl with cerebral palsy should have been watched 24/7. You don't deserve the children you have.'

Coral and I had received literally thousands of letters from members of the public and I can probably count on one hand those which were anything less than completely sympathetic to our distress. Yet no matter how many people contacted us wishing to express their condolences for the loss of April, it was always letters like these that stuck in our heads.

Countless people – our families, friends, the police, our counsellors and other bereaved parents like Sara Payne – had continually told us that we weren't to blame for what had happened. April was taken because she came into contact with an evil and depraved man, they reminded us, not because we were bad parents. Still, it was hard not to let cruel words like these get to us and leave us wondering if we'd really done everything in our power to protect our little girl. With the benefit of hindsight, we've realised that these letter-writers are cowards with empty lives. None of them seem brave enough to put their names to their vitriol and anyone who finds time to needlessly goad a grieving family has to take a long, hard look at themselves before dishing out accusations.

'My emotions are everywhere today,' I wrote that evening. 'I just find myself wanting to cry all day. I'm so lost. I don't know what to do and I have no goal in life now April is gone and I feel useless because of my eyesight. I'm just running on my love for April and hers for me, as well as my love for Coral, Jazmin and Harley. But I wonder, is love enough? I'm buckling and twisting under the pressure. I'm crying at the smallest things again. I'm just depressed and I want my girl back. I want to hear her sing, to give her a cuddle and look into those two, lovely brown eyes.

'I love you, April. Dad xxx.'

My mood was lifted the next day when the Sunday edition of the *Sun* released a link to our petition, along with a big article about the campaign. It featured coverage of Coral's meeting with Sara and they'd also included a link to the video they'd recorded on the website. I hoped it would encourage more people to take notice of what we were trying to do.

I thought it would be a good idea for us all to get out for a bit, so Coral, Jazmin and I went to New Quay to visit my mum and Dai, while Harley stayed at home and played with his friends. It was nice to get out and enjoy the good weather and we went for a coffee and a sandwich. I suggested we all go to the beach but Coral quickly vetoed the idea. It was a different beach from the one we'd visited the previous day with the photographer but we'd had so many happy afternoons there with April that she just found it too painful.

I noticed that Coral had thrown herself into the campaign and seemed permanently glued to her phone or the laptop. I worried that she may be doing too much too soon, but she insisted she was fine and, in a way, it was good for her to have a focus.

The next day we went shopping in the town and were stopped numerous times. It was the first time many people had seen us since the trial and they all wanted to hug and kiss us. While we appreciated the gestures, it was a little unnerving for Coral, who had become extremely claustrophobic. My mind flashed back to the day we went Christmas shopping in Aberystwyth and how panicked she had been when a stranger wanted to hug her. Thankfully these were all people we recognised and she coped well considering. We then took Harley to the cinema to see *Too Fast Too Furious 6*, which he loved.

'It's good to get out and try and be a normal family,' I wrote that night. 'But deep down, we will never be normal again. Sometimes I find myself staring at April's school photo or a small photo of her we have in the kitchen, which I like, and I just cry for a while. I'm lost and I don't really know quite why I'm crying but the tears just overflow and pour down my face.

'April, your mum is keeping to her word and trying to help others, keeping your name out there for a good cause. I'm trying my best to help your mum and look after her, Jazz, Harley, Autumn and Storm, as I promised. I love you, beautiful, and miss you so much. Driven by love, I can't fail.

'Love, Dad xxx.'

12

Downing Street

A fortnight after the end of the trial, we received a phone call from Ryan at the *Sun*, who asked if we would be interested in travelling to Downing Street to meet the Conservative MP Claire Perry to speak about our campaign. Claire Perry was a mother-of-three who had been elected to the House of Commons in 2010, after giving up a career in banking to enter politics. Since then, she'd enjoyed a meteoric rise to prominence and was now an adviser to the Prime Minister, David Cameron, with a specific interest in online child protection.

Although the meeting would involve another exhausting trip to London, we immediately agreed to attend. We'd been told that government ministers were due to meet with internet service providers within the next few weeks and we wanted the chance to have our say before then.

As is often the case with MPs, the meeting with Claire Perry was arranged rather hastily for the afternoon of Friday 14 June 2013. The *Sun* only managed to confirm the details late on the Thursday afternoon, so Coral and I had to hurriedly pack some bags and jump on the 6 p.m. train to Birmingham, where we'd catch our connection to London Euston.

We arrived in London around 10.30 p.m. and took a taxi to our hotel. The traffic was terrible and we were both tired and hungry, but luckily we had a very amiable driver who introduced himself to us as Larry.

'So, what brings you to London, then?' he asked us. We'd jumped into the back of the cab and he'd driven off without looking properly at our faces. It was obvious that he assumed we were tourists.

'We're going to Downing Street tomorrow,' I told him. 'Our daughter was taken away by a paedophile last year and we want to see if there's anything we can do to stop child porn on the internet.'

I thought Larry might crash into the car in front of him as he spun round to take a good look at us. Thankfully the roads were so congested we were moving at a snail's pace. Surveying our faces, I saw an expression of awful realisation spread across his face.

'I'm so sorry,' he said, quietly. I sensed genuine pity in his voice. 'I didn't recognise you there.'

'Don't worry about it,' I replied. We were so used to being stopped by strangers that it made a nice change.

'All the taxi drivers have been talking about this,' he went on. 'We think it's amazing, what you're doing. We're right behind you.'

It was 11.30 p.m. when we got to our hotel and I tried to press a handful of notes into Larry's hand, but he waved them away.

'Put the fare towards the garden you've been building for April,' he said.

'What a lovely bloke,' I said to Coral, as he drove away. It was nice to hear first-hand how much public support we had.

We quickly grabbed some food before heading to bed, but I couldn't sleep. I tossed and turned for a few hours before it was time to get up. Ryan met us shortly before noon and we sat in the hotel lobby discussing what the meeting would involve.

Ryan explained that we wouldn't be the only family in the meeting. Natalie Sharp, whose twelve-year-old daughter Tia had been murdered two months before April's disappearance, would also be attending with her boyfriend, David Niles.

Tia was reported missing on 3 August 2012, after apparently vanishing from the home of her grandmother, Christine Bicknell, in New Addington, near Croydon, South London. The previous evening, Christine's partner Stuart Hazell had been babysitting Tia while Christine worked a night shift at a local care home. Hazell told the police that Tia had gone to buy shoes at a shopping centre five miles away and failed to return.

The police searched for Tia for a week and Hazell, a window cleaner, feigned devastation. He even attended a candlelit vigil wearing a T-shirt emblazoned with her picture and the word 'missing' and was supported by relatives as he appeared to break down. But, unbeknown to Tia's family, Hazell had developed an unhealthy interest in child pornography in the months leading up to her disappearance. He had downloaded countless illegal images, which he kept on a memory card hidden behind a door frame in the kitchen. Most of the children pictured were pre-pubescent girls and Hazell seemed to have a particular interest in girls who, like Tia, wore glasses.

However, on 10 August, police found a body in a bag in Christine's loft, wrapped in a black sheet. It had already begun to decompose and a post-mortem later confirmed it belonged to Tia. An exact cause of death was never established, but police said she was most likely to have been suffocated.

Hazell was arrested and charged with Tia's murder the next day. The police later discovered that, while he pretended to be distraught in front of television cameras, Hazell had continued to access illegal incest websites on his phone. He had also taken pictures of Tia's body, naked and in a sexual pose.

The following May, he went on trial at the Old Bailey in London, just over a week after the case against Mark Bridger began at Mold Crown Court. However, after five days, Hazell changed his plea from not guilty to guilty and was sentenced to life imprisonment, with a minimum term of thirty-eight years. The judge, Mr Justice Nicol, confirmed that Hazell's semen was found in the room where Tia slept. Tia's DNA had also been discovered on a sexual device in the bedroom Hazell shared with her grandmother.

Coral and I were both shocked by the parallels between Hazell and Bridger. We were particularly alarmed by how easily Hazell appeared to have accessed illegal images using the browser on his mobile phone. Some of the search terms he used were 'naked little girlies', 'illegal underage incest pics' and 'daddy daughter pictures' – all of which returned results.

Tia had idolised Hazell, even calling him Granddad, and her

family had trusted him to look after her. But, fuelled by the filth he was able to access with just a few clicks, he began to descend into depravity. When Tia vanished, no one had any idea that Hazell had been gripped by this dangerous obsession, or that he'd been secretly filming Tia in her underwear whenever she had a sleepover at her grandmother's. Like Bridger, he was not known to the police for offending against children and outwardly showed no signs of a sexual interest in young girls. The only way anyone could have foretold what these monsters were capable of was by looking at their internet history – but no one ever did.

It was devastating for Coral and me to hear that another family had gone through such similar events but it only increased our determination to do something about it. Would Bridger and Hazell have gone on to do such awful things to April and Tia if they hadn't been able to get their hands on such sick material? Would the police have investigated them sooner if they'd been alerted to what these men were searching for? Since the trial, we'd begun asking ourselves these questions on an almost hourly basis. We'd never be certain, but we wanted to do everything in our power to make sure other parents didn't have to go through the nightmare of wondering what might have been.

Ryan had arranged for a taxi to pick us up at the hotel around 12.40 p.m. and we were driven to the back entrance of 10 Downing Street, which was being manned by two armed guards. Natalie and David were waiting for us and we said a polite hello, before being allowed in. I was thankful that the guards used their common sense and didn't try to search us, as I knew that this would have made Coral anxious and claustrophobic.

I'd often seen the front of 10 Downing Street on television, but

I had no idea how grand its interior would be. Everywhere we turned we were greeted by sweeping staircases, crystal chandeliers and marble pillars. It was like entering another world. A year ago, I would have been extremely nervous about being in the home of the Prime Minister. Now our family had been through so much that nothing could faze me.

A photographer then took us to the front entrance, where Coral, Natalie, David and I posed for pictures. Afterwards, we were taken upstairs to a conference room where Claire Perry was waiting.

She rose to greet us and the first thing I noticed was how tall and elegant she was – she must have been at least six feet tall. She was very personable and charismatic, shaking hands with David and me and hugging Natalie and Coral before we sat down to chat.

It soon became obvious that Natalie was a bit more extroverted than us, and she quickly became very animated when she was asked for her opinion on how we could best combat child abuse online.

'I want to see a change in the law in our innocent angels' names,' she told Claire. 'Those little girls just cannot die in vain. This has happened twice now, to Tia and to April. Not again. Never again.'

She then made the point about how alike the cases were and Coral and I found ourselves nodding in agreement – it was truly frightening.

'We don't want there to be a third, fourth and fifth family sitting in here in the same situation because we haven't moved and done anything,' I added.

'Your sacrifices won't be in vain,' Claire said, before telling us she would give David Cameron some feedback on our meeting.

Ryan and the photographer then left the four of us alone with Claire, so we could have a private conversation. Natalie became very tearful when she spoke about Tia's funeral and this seemed to set Coral off. We still hadn't been able to make preparations for April's funeral and, until we'd said our final farewell, it seemed like our lives were still on hold.

'We haven't even got a body,' Coral sobbed. 'Just a few small skull bones.'

I placed my hand over hers, before Claire took her in her arms and gave her a hug. There was a quiet, respectful silence for a few minutes before we continued with our discussion.

'There needs to be zero tolerance on indecent images,' I said, once we'd all composed ourselves. 'We think there should be dedicated policing of the internet to make sure this happens.'

David, who had been fairly silent until now, nodded and said it was unthinkable that another family should go through the pain we'd all experienced.

'We're all right behind you,' Claire said. Although she'd been very sympathetic to us and had said all the right things, I had to force myself to remember that she was still a politician. Words were meaningless – it was action we needed.

'That's rare for MPs,' I replied. 'Will you be able to keep us up to date with what's happening?'

Claire agreed and we were taken back downstairs and out through the back of the house. On the way to our taxi, we walked through the garden where David Cameron often made televised speeches. I recognised it instantly, as I'd seen various Prime Ministers address the nation from the same spot over the years. Before April was taken, I might have been excited to see such an iconic place but now it was just yet another painful reminder that we'd never be mixing with such rich and powerful people if we hadn't lost our daughter.

A few days later, Channel 5 News contacted us to ask if we would give a televised interview on online child protection. The interview would be filmed to coincide with the summit the government had organised with major internet providers on the issue. Now we'd spoken to Claire Perry, Coral and I had privately agreed that we'd like to meet David Cameron, to discuss the issue with him. We would use the interview to appeal to him for a meeting.

One of the presenters, Tessa Chapman, came to the house and asked us a few questions about the campaign. After all the travelling we'd been doing it was nice to do the interview in more comfortable surroundings. Coral and I settled ourselves on the couch and we each fixed a pink bow to our shirts. Tessa was very friendly and sympathetic and made us feel at ease.

'Do you think that the access Mark Bridger had to these images created the man he was?' she asked us, once the cameras had started rolling.

'I do,' Coral replied. 'He got all these things up on the computer and, a few hours later, our little one had disappeared.'

'It certainly fuelled somebody who was in that frame of mind,' I agreed. 'Anyone else who is thinking of children in this way, these images will only set them off.'

'During the summit that is happening today, the government

will essentially ask internet providers and search engines to police themselves,' Tessa said. 'Do you think they need to be forced to do more?'

'They need to do a lot more but everybody needs to do something,' I replied. 'It's not just Google and the search engines. If an individual stumbles upon something online, they should report it. Tia Sharp and April's cases were linked to the internet and they happened within a few months of each other. If these things don't get sorted out, this is just going to escalate. Mark Bridger downloaded 400 images and nothing was flagged up.'

'He had all these images and nobody realised,' Coral said. 'Not even the police. No one.'

'They came off several sites,' I went on. 'It's very hard to believe that the big internet companies could let that happen.'

'It makes me furious,' Coral said. 'Words can't express how mad I am. It's disgusting what happened and how he got these pictures. The companies that allow them should have a massive fine and the money should be put back into the police so they can carry on flagging people up. The people who do it should be charged and put on the Sex Offenders' Register.' She took a deep breath, before continuing. 'That list should be made public – not their addresses, just their names – so people know who they are and what they've done.'

Tessa then asked us a few questions about April. We both found it relatively easy to talk about the campaign, as we'd become so passionate about it, but speaking about what we'd lost and why we were here was when it got tough.

'April was a fighter in life and this will be her last fight,' I told Tessa. 'In death.' I said the last two words slowly and carefully. It was still so hard to accept April was gone forever. 'I hope it will be a legacy for her.'

'April was a fighter from the word go,' Coral added. 'And I promised her I would do this for her.' By now her voice was breaking and she was struggling to contain her emotions. 'I said I'd help other children so another family doesn't have to go through this.'

She began to cry, so I took her hand in mine, willing her to go on.

'It's not just us,' she sobbed. 'It's their brothers and sisters. It affects them, too. I think the government should put more pressure on these companies because I promised April I would fight. If people see something that isn't right, they should contact the police so these people can get some help themselves before another child is killed or abused. I'd like to get David Cameron involved as he could be an ambassador for this fight.'

'So you want to meet David Cameron?' Tessa asked.

'Yes, I'd like to meet him and put our points through to him,' Coral said. 'Paul and I would like his help. He's a dad, too. We'd like him to back us and help get the law changed in April's name.'

At the same time, Tia Sharp's biological father, Steven Carter, was interviewed in the Channel 5 studio in London by another presenter, Emma Crosby. Although we had never met him in person, we were heartened to hear that he agreed wholeheartedly with our views on online child protection. He, too, believed the government needed to work with the internet companies to find a solution to the problem.

'We will never get over what happened,' he said, during his interview. 'All we can do is prevent this from happening again.'

'As a bereaved parent, what do you want David Cameron to do?' Emma asked him.

'He needs to ban it,' he replied. 'There should be no opportunity for these people to set up pages or put these images on the internet. If we're able to trace IP addresses, why aren't we tracing these people who are doing this?'

Little did we know how seriously Channel 5 News would take our fight. The following day, a journalist from the programme was covering the G8 Summit in Lough Erne in Northern Ireland, where David Cameron was meeting with other world leaders. He was allowed just a few minutes to speak to the Prime Minister and chose to ask him if he'd be willing to meet us. The Prime Minister agreed in principle. A few weeks later, we received a call from the *Sun,* who had also been pressing for a meeting. One of their reporters had managed to get David Cameron's office to commit to spending a morning with us on Friday 19 July.

Of course, this presented us with a bit of a dilemma. Both Channel 5 News and the *Sun* wanted exclusive access to the meeting and our loyalties were divided, as we believed they'd both played an equal part in helping make it happen. We wanted as much coverage of the campaign as possible to raise awareness of what we were trying to achieve, but we knew we needed to keep the various media outlets we'd worked with on our side if we wanted to make as big an impact as we could. There were lots of crossed wires and confusion, which made an already stressful situation more stressful as we didn't know much about managing the media. Eventually, after a few fraught phone calls, the *Sun* and Channel 5 News agreed they would both attend. We were glad they were willing to cooperate.

We got to London around 7 p.m. the night before the meeting but it was a blisteringly hot evening and we found it hard to sleep in our hotel room, even with the air conditioning. We got up early and some chaperones from the *Sun* were waiting for us in the hotel lobby, along with Natalie and David, who would also attend the meeting.

We had a few pictures taken, before being ushered through security and upstairs into the same room where we had met Claire Perry a few weeks previously. The *Sun* took photographs and Channel 5 News did some filming, before they left us alone with the Prime Minister.

David Cameron spoke very gently to us. He addressed us by name, listened intently to everything we said and made all of the right noises. But, like Claire Perry, he was a true politician, and he never fully committed to anything.

I asked him how likely it was that the government would pass a law which would make internet companies liable for huge fines if they allowed people access to images depicting child abuse.

'Everyone knows the Tia and April stories,' I told him. 'We never want another family sitting here having suffered the same thing.'

'This is an incredibly difficult thing to get right,' he said, meeting my gaze. 'We are looking across the board – nothing is ruled out, including passing laws. There's not enough being done to find these images and those responsible for putting them there. That should be step one and we are going to do more of that.'

I asked him how they planned to deal with the search engines which were allowing these images to be shared.

'Targeting firms that let people upload the pictures is crucial,' the Prime Minister said. 'But the problem is there are some words that you might put in with an innocent explanation that can lead to horrible images.' He paused for a moment. 'Then there are people – including the hideous killers you have come face to face with – who are putting in appalling words to get appalling images.'

'If a website is reported, its IP address should be blocked,' I replied, firmly. 'Why can't they take this stuff off the internet? Kids are getting killed, raped, abused and messed up for the rest of their lives. What's their excuse? I think it's money. They have the technology and they can do this. If we could get a law for Europe, then that would be a good start.'

'It's a triangle,' Natalie added. 'The people uploading it, the people letting them upload it, and the people looking for it.'

We chatted for around half an hour in total. The Prime Minister promised us he would try and influence the big internet companies using diplomacy. If that didn't work, he told us, he would consider looking at passing a law.

We'd always known that this meeting wouldn't provide an instant solution to the problem but when the Prime Minister left – shaking our hands firmly as he exited the room – we were left wondering if he had really taken our concerns on board or whether he was simply paying us lip service. Every day that action was delayed was another day paedophiles were free to trawl the internet for the depraved images like those which led to April and Tia's deaths. We were desperate to prevent another tragedy but it was like a ticking time bomb.

'The clock is ticking against him,' I told James Beal, the *Sun* reporter who'd accompanied us, once the Prime Minister had gone. 'Every day it's delayed there are more people getting fuelled up on this. It would break my heart if someone was in this situation again.'

We then had another brief meeting with Claire Perry. Coral and I told her someone had posted a picture of a child with a huge inflatable penis on one of April's Facebook sites and that it had taken Jamzin just five minutes to find it. She looked completely taken aback and we could tell she didn't quite know what to say.

We then got a taxi back to our hotel, where we had a quick debrief with the *Sun* before heading to catch our train home. As ever, coming home to a house without April in it was heartbreaking. Coral went to visit friends, while I took the dogs for a walk up the hill where I'd tied my ribbons. I couldn't stop the tears and it was a few hours before I found the strength to go back home again. As I sat crying with my head in my hands, it was hard to believe I'd been sat across from the most powerful man in the country just a few hours earlier. Our lives had become unrecognisable, even to us.

'Running around is very tiring,' I wrote that evening. 'It takes a few days to recover. I'm very emotional and I find myself tearful for a few days but then I tend to be OK(ish). It hurts me to think about what should have been but isn't because of one cruel man.

'I love you, April. Dad xxx.'

A few days later, David Cameron made a speech at a conference organised by the children's charity NSPCC. We didn't get a chance to hear it in full until a few days later, but we'd got to grips with its main points before Channel 5 News called round to ask for our reaction to it.

In short, the Prime Minister said that major search engines such as Google, Yahoo and Bing would have three months to introduce stricter measures to block child abuse images online. Experts from the Child Exploitation and Online Protection Centre would be given more powers to examine secretive file-sharing networks and there would also be a database of banned images to help police track paedophiles.

'There are some searches which are so abhorrent, where it's absolutely obvious the person at the keyboard is looking for revolting child abuse images,' the Prime Minister had told conference delegates.

'In these cases, there should be no search results returned at all. Put simply, there needs to be a list of terms, a blacklist, which offer up no direct search returns.

'So I have a very clear message for Google, Bing, Yahoo! and the rest: you have a duty to act on this, and it is a moral duty. I simply don't accept the argument that some of these companies have used, to say that these searches should be allowed because of freedom of speech.

'On Friday I sat with the parents of Tia Sharp and April Jones. They want to feel that everyone involved is doing everything they can to play their full part in helping rid the internet of child abuse images. So I've called for a progress report in Downing Street in October with the search engines coming in to update me.'

For me, it was difficult to know how to feel. On the one hand, this seemed like a step in the right direction but, on the other, it felt like so much more could be done. David Cameron had essentially given these companies a stay of execution until October and it was still only July. Was he bowing down to these companies because of how much money they had? Both Coral and I knew how quickly Bridger's vile obsession had got out of hand. We could only hope that history didn't repeat itself between now and then.

'It's not enough,' Coral said, emphatically. 'If we don't start fining them, this will happen again. He's being too soft on them.'

On Channel 5 News that evening, Emma Crosby grilled the Prime Minister on his speech, asking him if he was really convinced he'd been tough enough on the internet companies.

'Will you be able to look Coral and Paul Jones in the eye in eighteen months and say you've done everything you can?' she asked, pointedly.

'I'll be able to look them in the eye and say we've taken some good steps forward,' he replied, carefully. 'I don't think we will have done everything that some campaigners will want, but I think we will have made lots of really big steps down the road that will help parents, that will help children and that will reduce the amount of child abuse that takes place and is posted online.'

She then asked him how the discussions with the companies involved had been.

'Of course they've been heated, because these are important issues,' he admitted. 'I'm not trying to get into a massive great fight with a bunch of businesses. We talked to them about what is possible and we made some really good steps forward.'

Channel 5 News had also asked some of the internet companies for their reaction to what the Prime Minister had said. Perhaps predictably, none of them wanted to give interviews on the subject. We thought their silence was extremely cowardly. What did they have to hide from us?

Coral was very emotional in our own interview and it was hard for me to watch. Once the camera crew had left, she admitted to me that she felt David Cameron had used some of our words and ideas but wasn't willing to properly take on the might of such big, powerful businesses.

However, we were slowly coming to realise that, in politics, nothing moves quickly. I remembered our meeting with Sara Payne and how long she'd fought for Sarah's Law. We had a long road ahead of us. In a few short weeks, we'd made some progress but the fight was only just beginning. We'd done as much research as we could and we were trying to keep our heads above water with all of the technical terms and jargon but, no matter how hard it got, we wouldn't give up.

'I don't understand why everything takes so long,' Coral said, exasperated. 'If this had happened in an MP's family I bet they wouldn't be taking their time over it.'

'I know,' I replied. 'We'll just have to hope that they do what's right eventually.'

Before April was taken, we'd have laughed in the face of anyone who suggested we'd one day be sharing a table with some of the country's most powerful people, speaking about a political campaign. It was never a life we would have chosen for ourselves – we were hundreds of miles from Westminster and the hustle and bustle of parliament in more ways than one. Travelling exhausted us and we weren't impressed by fancy restaurants and posh hotels. We'd both have chosen a quiet walk along the beach with the children over hobnobbing with politicians any day. But, now, we didn't feel like we had a choice. This path had been chosen for us.

That evening, I opened April's bedroom door and felt the tears sting my eyes.

'This is all for you, April,' I said softly.

13

The House of Horrors

While we tried to focus on our campaign against child pornography, we also had to think about picking up the pieces of our lives. We might have looked like we were holding it together to the outside world, but behind closed doors it was a very different story.

Sara Payne has often said that she felt like two people in the aftermath of her daughter's death. In public, she was the brave bereaved mother, the campaigner who was determined to do anything she could to stop another family going through the hell that hers had been – but once the television cameras had stopped rolling, she could barely bring herself to get out of bed. We were beginning to understand exactly what she meant.

Sir Richard Branson, the chairman of Virgin, had read about April's death and kindly offered us a free family holiday to

Orlando, Florida. We were very grateful to him and it was good for us to get away and spend some quality time together as a family, away from the distractions of home.

We hadn't bargained for how hot and humid Florida would be in the middle of August, though. It was peak season, as it was the school holidays in so many places all over the world, and the parks were extremely crowded. Coral struggled to cope with the congestion, although she tried to put a brave face on in front of the children, who seemed to be enjoying themselves.

When we arrived home, the local council was renovating all the houses on Bryn-y-Gog and our kitchen had been ripped out. Of course, we'd had lots of advance warning that this would be happening, but coming home to such upheaval only served to make us even more stressed and tearful. Perhaps now all the hype surrounding us was dying down, we had more time to be alone with our thoughts.

'Over the last week I've struggled with my emotions,' I wrote in my diary, a few days after we arrived home. 'I've been very tired today. Coral has been very down as well – a mixture of jet lag and the house being turned upside down as our kitchen is being refitted. It's also been very quiet. Not many people are calling and we feel a little let down – now the show is over, we're on our own.

'I walked my dogs up over the hill today and cried at the top. I think it's my place to let off steam and just think and have a cry. I've been crying most nights lately. Sometimes just a few tears, sometimes a lot.

'I love you, April. Dad xxx.'

*

Around this time, Coral decided to go to the doctor. She was already on strong medication for depression but her situation was becoming intolerable. She'd always been so fiercely independent but, almost a year on, simply leaving the house filled her with dread. She couldn't go anywhere on her own and she was fast becoming a prisoner in her own home.

After a few appointments, she was diagnosed with agoraphobia. We were glad we at least knew what the problem was, but the diagnosis didn't provide a miracle solution. Instead we both continued to see our counsellors, knowing that this would at least help us sort through the messy thoughts that continued to live in our heads.

It was at this point that I decided to stop writing in my diary every day. It had been a lifeline for me throughout the investigation and the trial, but I began to realise that forcing myself to write every evening was making me pick over old thoughts, often unnecessarily. I couldn't bear to throw it away, but I decided to keep it in a drawer so I could still write if I felt the need, or if there were any major developments.

I suppose I was beginning to come to terms with the idea that we might never get closure. It was highly unlikely that Bridger would tell us where the rest of April's remains were and it was even more unlikely that he'd ever admit what really happened on the night she vanished.

Early on in the investigation, Coral had asked Dave and Hayley if there was any possibility we could visit Bridger's house. April had almost certainly died there and my wife thought it would help her feel closer to our daughter.

I wasn't so sure. After we'd seen the pictures of the cottage in the lead-up to the trial, with the arrows pointing to the spots where traces of April's blood had been found, I'd imagined the hundreds of horrific things that could have happened within those four walls. I had no desire to see the cottage for myself, but I knew how important it was to Coral and there was no way I'd let her go there alone.

We'd first asked our FLOs about this just after Christmas but the final decision rested with Andy John. He'd asked us to hold off until the trial was over, as the house was still a crime scene and he didn't want to risk contaminating it. He was also concerned that we might be called as witnesses and, if we'd been allowed to see key evidence before the court case, Bridger's lawyers could argue that he hadn't had a fair trial.

Once the court case was over, we raised the issue again. There were still some legal issues that had to be resolved and the police couldn't give us access to the house until Bridger decided whether or not to appeal his conviction. However, a few weeks after we returned from Florida, we got a call from Dave, who told us that we'd now be able to take a trip to Mount Pleasant if we wished. Keen to get it over with, we arranged to go with him to the cottage later that same week.

On the morning of the visit, I woke up feeling uneasy. We'd been trying not to think about Bridger since the trial had ended and we didn't even like mentioning his name, unless it was in the context of our campaign against child pornography.

The only time we'd really had a proper discussion about him was a few weeks previously. We'd been at the cinema in Aberystwyth to watch a film called *After Earth* with the children. The film was just about to start when Coral's mobile had rung with a call from Hayley. Hayley had wanted to tell us that Bridger had been attacked in prison by another inmate. She was concerned that the newspapers would pick up on the story and that we would read about it before the police had a chance to speak to us.

After the trial, Bridger had been taken to a high-security prison in Wakefield, West Yorkshire. Rumour had it that the other prisoners had been speaking about an attack against him for some time, as they thought it might force him to reveal what he'd done with April's body.

In the end, it was a fellow inmate called Juvinal Ferreira who took matters into his own hands and slashed Bridger from his temple to his chin using a knife fashioned from a razor. Ferreira had severed one of Bridger's arteries and he had required surgery, as well as thirty stitches. Hayley told Coral that it was likely he'd be scarred for life.

When Coral came back into the cinema, you'd have been forgiven for thinking she was a football fan whose favourite team had just won the FA Cup.

'Yes!' she shouted. People were staring and pointing, but she didn't care. 'Paul, someone's got him! Someone's attacked him in prison!' Realising how loud she'd been, she turned to the people sitting next to us and mouthed 'sorry', as she shuffled back into her seat.

'Well, I can't say I'm too upset about that,' I whispered, as the opening credits flashed up. Needless to say, I didn't have to ask who she was referring to.

Of course, under most circumstances we didn't condone violence and Juvinal Ferreira was himself a dangerous offender who'd been convicted of murder and rape. Two wrongs didn't make a right, and even if Bridger was attacked a thousand times it wouldn't bring April back.

Yet it was impossible to have any sort of compassion for a man who had obviously inflicted such pain and suffering on our little girl and shown no remorse. He deserved to feel at least a fraction of the pain we had to live with every day. Some readers might not agree with our attitude, but I'd challenge any parent to react differently when faced with the same situation. I've never been a malicious or nasty person but, as I lay in bed trying to mentally prepare for our visit to his house, I found myself wishing the next attack would be even worse. It was frightening what terrible thoughts this man could make me have.

I prepared breakfast and got Coral up a few hours before Dave was due to collect us at 10.30 a.m. Neither my wife nor I could eat or say much. Dave already had the keys to the cottage, as he'd arranged to pick them up from Andy the previous day and, when I heard the sound of his car engine outside the house, I was gripped by an overwhelming desire to run outside and tell him it was all off, that I'd changed my mind. How could we cope, seeing the spot where this animal had laid our daughter on the floor, bleeding and dying, like a piece of rubbish? It was madness. What were we thinking?

Of course, I didn't tell Dave to cancel the visit. I took one look at Coral and the pained desperation in her eyes, and I knew this was something I had to do, if not for myself, then for her. I wasn't sure if the visit would give her any peace of mind but I understood that she couldn't even attempt to move on until she'd seen the place where our little girl had likely breathed her last.

I let Dave in through the back door and we quickly gathered our things. It wasn't a time for preamble or small talk.

'Ready to go?' he asked, his tone soft but solemn. In unison, we nodded.

'Yes,' I replied. 'Let's get this over with.'

Coral and I both climbed into the back seat. Normally one of us would have got in the front with Dave but I wanted to be close to my wife so I could comfort her if she became upset on the way there. Hayley, a hardened police officer of many years standing, had been so affected the first time she'd visited the cottage a few weeks into the investigation that she'd had to take the next day off. I could only imagine what it would do to us as April's parents.

The mood was sombre and none of us said much in the car as Bryn-y-Gog disappeared behind us. I was already thinking about April's last journey in Bridger's car, particularly as we passed the petrol station on the edge of Machynlleth where a witness had seen his Land Rover speed past shortly after she'd vanished. What was our little girl thinking, as she was driven along these leafy, remote country roads to her death? The sun would have been setting and she would have known it was getting close to her bedtime. Had she asked to go home or turn back? Nausea consumed me as I imagined Bridger pulling over in some deserted layby to abuse her, his mind warped by the filth he'd been devouring as he sat alone at his laptop. April was so trusting and naive that I hoped with all of my heart that she'd been oblivious to what was about to happen to her.

There are two ways to drive between Machynlleth and Ceinws, and the police believed that Bridger had taken the most direct route, along the main A487 road. They surmised that he'd have wanted to get as far from Machynlleth as he could as soon as possible to avoid detection.

'Let's take the back road,' Dave said, with a quick glance in the rear-view mirror. It was like he'd seen the pain etched on my face and read my mind. Knowing that we were about to see the house where our daughter breathed her last was awful enough – being driven on the exact route Bridger had taken her to meet her end might have pushed us over the edge.

Dave slowed to a crawl as we approached the single-track road which led to the village. I reached for Coral's hand and knotted my fingers through hers as the car edged along the stony path. It was only then I realised how sweaty my palms were. Coral's face was white and she was shaking slightly, but I could see the determination in her eyes. She had to do this.

As the small scattering of cottages came into view, I couldn't help but think how strange it was that this tiny settlement had become one of the most photographed sites in the UK over the past year, splashed all over the pages of newspapers for weeks on end. Hidden in the depths of the valley of the River Dulas, passers-by would barely have noticed its existence before this horrible tragedy took place. Even we, as locals, rarely had any reason to come here. I'd had a friend who'd lived here many years previously, and I'd visited him a few times, but we'd never come here as a family and it certainly wouldn't have been a place April would have recognised.

Barely more than a dozen houses were visible from the road. Perhaps the only sign of life was a small pub called Tafarn Dwynant, which relied on the custom of bikers and walkers. Most of the locals were elderly and it wasn't unheard of for a year or two to pass without a single crime being committed here. But now its anonymity was gone forever.

I inhaled sharply as Mount Pleasant appeared on the horizon. The whitewashed cottage stood apart from the other houses and my stomach knotted as I caught sight of the chimney. It looked just as it had in the newspaper pictures, except now the grass outside it had become thick and overgrown.

Dave pulled up in front of the house. Without speaking, we all got out.

The lock was stiff and Dave had to give the door a good push before it swung open. I was immediately overwhelmed by the putrid smell of damp. It was the middle of August, but the house was deathly cold. Both Coral and I shuddered as we walked over the threshold. I wasn't sure if it was the temperature or what we were about to see that prompted this reaction. It was probably a combination of both. Still in silence, we walked into the lounge. I hardly noticed that all the furniture had been removed.

All I could focus on was the fireplace.

The carpet had been ripped out and there was a big piece of Perspex on the hearth, covering the spot where April's blood had been found. I found myself walking towards it, but Coral seemed frozen to the spot, next to Dave. I followed my wife's eyes as they travelled from the fireplace to the Perspex cover and back again.

'Can I have a look upstairs?' Coral asked Dave. It was the first time anyone had spoken since we'd walked through the door.

'If you like,' he replied. I didn't go with them. I needed a few minutes alone.

Coral recalls:

By the time we were taken to the cottage, I'd for months been consumed by the desire to visit Mount Pleasant. I was never quite sure why, or what it would achieve. I just knew I had to do it.

Nervous anticipation had been pumping through my body as we'd walked through the door. We were only a fifteen-minute drive from Bryn-y-Gog but Bridger's isolated cottage seemed like a million miles away from our warm family home. With its unkempt, overgrown garden and unmistakable aroma of damp, it had the air of a house that wasn't meant to be lived in.

I wondered if my little girl had still been conscious when she'd arrived here in the depths of the countryside. If she'd been aware of what was happening, she must have felt so lost and alone, as darkness fell around this bleak house. Would we ever know if she had been crying for Paul and me?

I was shaking as I stepped inside, but I wasn't sure if it was because I was nervous or because of how cold it was. I looked at the fire and tried to compose myself, as I allowed myself to think about the last time it would have been lit, nearly eleven months previously.

I was strangely calm as my eyes wandered to the Perspex sheet covering the area of the floor where April's blood had been found. I knew instinctively the grief and anger would hit me in a day or so, and the gravity of it all would be so debilitating that I probably wouldn't leave the house for days. But, for the moment, it seemed like my body had been shocked into a strange numbness.

I'm not sure why I wanted to go upstairs. Dave and Hayley had told us that there was no evidence from the forensic teams to suggest that April had been on the top floor of the house, but I felt the need to comb every corner just in case there was some cryptic clue as to what had really happened to my little girl. After all, I was her mum. If I couldn't find the answers, who could?

As I climbed the stairs, my sore knees weak with the effort, I didn't know what I was looking for. Another chill ran through my body as Dave opened the door to the first bedroom. Unlike the bottom floor, its furniture was still in place. It was, I could only assume, almost exactly as Bridger had left it when he'd walked into Machynlleth with the pretence of joining the search for April.

The bed was unmade and there were clothes lying all over the floor. What had he been thinking, I wondered, as he nodded off to sleep that terrible October night? Had he already been piecing together the ridiculous cover stories he'd use time and time again in the months to come? He was so callous he'd probably slept like a log, while I clung to my daughter's teddies in her empty bed and Paul paced the living room floor, delirious with worry.

The second bedroom was even more of a tip. Bridger had only lived in the cottage for five weeks and it was obvious he hadn't attempted to make it look homely. There was a horrible, stale smell and his belongings were scattered everywhere without a second thought for his children, who regularly visited him and probably had to sleep in this disgusting excuse for a spare bedroom.

I stood still for a moment, allowing my eyes to sweep the room, but it was hopeless. There was nothing here that could tell me anything about April. She probably hadn't even been in either of these rooms.

Dave then took me downstairs to the bathroom. There were little green arrows on the wall and we already knew that these pointed to the positions where spots of April's blood had been traced. There was also an arrow on the shower curtain and on the bathroom door.

It was nothing I wasn't expecting. We'd seen plenty of pictures of this room before and during the trial. Yet I still find it hard to put into words how it felt being there in the flesh. Was my little girl dead as Bridger carried her maimed body through here, or was she still dying? I was gripped by an agonising realisation that I'd probably never find out. It broke my heart to think of April suffering but I still craved answers as to what had happened to her. I'd tried to convince myself that visiting Mount Pleasant would give me some closure, but I knew in that moment that I'd never get closure as long as I lived. Bridger hadn't just snatched our precious girl from the street and murdered her in cold blood; he'd flatly refused to tell us what had really happened, or what he'd done with her, and that was a whole different crime in itself.

My eyes fixed on the green arrows as I realised I'd be tortured by these awful thoughts until my dying day. The nightmares would never end and the tears would never stop flowing. It wasn't Mark Bridger who had the real life sentence – it was me.

*

While Coral and Dave had been upstairs, I'd wandered around the ground floor. I'd had a quick look in the bathroom and I'd seen the green arrows on the wall. Then I'd walked into the kitchen, where April's blood had been found on the washing machine. I hadn't known what to do next, so I'd gone back into the living room. Without the furniture, it looked much bigger than it had done in the pictures and I could see the marks on the floor where the carpet had been lifted before it was taken away by the forensic teams.

Without thinking, I knelt down on the floor next to the Perspex covering. Almost instinctively I put my hand on the cold, black fireplace and started to weep. My tears weren't the gasping, throaty sobs I often cried while walking in the hills. Instead they were respectful and almost silent. I wasn't sure how long I stayed there but it can't have been much more than fifteen minutes. I was relieved when Coral and Dave reappeared.

'Shall we go?' Dave asked, gently.

'Yes,' I replied, wiping my eyes as I clambered to my feet.

Coral and I didn't say much about Mount Pleasant on the journey home. I think it took us both a while to collect our thoughts, as it was few days before we had a proper conversation about it. In a way, we were glad we'd gone. Even I, for all my reluctance, had to admit that I'd had a gnawing curiosity about what lay inside Bridger's house. But it had far from given us answers. In some respects, it had just thrown up more excruciating questions.

14

April's Final Journey

After the trial, April's remains had been taken to Aberystwyth Police Station, as they couldn't be released to us for a funeral until the coroner's report had been concluded. The hearing was scheduled for 16 September 2013, meaning we'd have to wait almost four months before we could lay our daughter to rest.

However, we decided to begin planning for April's final farewell towards the end of August. We wanted it to be a perfect celebration of her short life and we knew it would take a lot of organisation. We wanted the service to be held in St Peter's Church in Machynlleth. Although we weren't religious as a family, the church and its vicar, Kath Rodgers, had shown us such kindness and support in the months since April was taken, that it seemed the most appropriate place to have the funeral.

We'd agreed that the press could attend the church but

decided on a private burial at the local graveyard to which only close friends and family would be invited. It was important that we kept some of the day for ourselves. We then planned to invite around 120 guests to a wake at the Celtica Visitor Centre. It seemed apt, as this was where so many people had congregated in the terrible first days of the search, desperate to help us find April. We extended this invitation to the police officers and mountain rescue teams as a gesture of gratitude for everything they'd done for us.

We arranged a meeting with a local undertaker, Dilwyn Rees. Dave came along with us, as it was important for the police to be represented. We knew to expect hundreds of mourners, not to mention the nation's press, and officers would have to close the roads surrounding the church in order to accommodate them.

Dilwyn was a kind man who told us he'd do everything in his power to make things perfect for us but the meeting was a tough one. We'd had eleven months to prepare ourselves for making these arrangements, but planning a funeral for our five-year-old child seemed unnatural and wrong. Coral was fairly quiet throughout and went straight to bed when we returned home. It was the middle of the afternoon, but she slept for almost six hours. Just after 10 p.m., I took her some coffee and a bowl of cereal and tentatively coaxed her to eat.

'I'm sorry,' she said, sadly. 'Today just knocked the stuffing out of me.'

It wasn't long before Coral had drifted off again and I found myself reaching for my diary. It was the first time in a while I'd put pen to paper but the funeral was throwing up lots of new emotions for me.

'Talking about April's funeral was difficult and emotional for me,' I wrote. 'It's the thought of organising it. How do you manage a funeral for your daughter, just five and a half years old? We have so little of her – just some dust and a few bits of bone. There isn't much to put to rest. We don't have much to show for our sweet and beautiful girl. It's hard, so damn hard. Some days you just get so beat up and stressed and tired.

'But I've had eleven months to prepare myself for this. Talking to my counsellors helps me a lot but Coral has only just started to talk and face up to the fact that April is dead and there will be a funeral. I only hope talking with the counsellors will help her like it has helped me. It doesn't make the pain go away, though – it's always there, that dull ache. A deep sadness washes over me every now and then and I feel like I'm back where we started and it's October 2012 all over again.

'I love you, April. Dad xxx '

A few days later, we decided on a date: Thursday 26 September, just five days shy of the first anniversary of April's disappearance. Coincidentally this was also my mum's birthday. We'd originally wanted to hold the service two days later, on the Saturday, but Kath was unavailable and it was important to us that she was there to conduct it. Dave and Hayley also advised us that a Saturday funeral would present more problems for the police from a logistical point of view.

A year before April had died, Coral had taken the children to Blackpool to celebrate Jazmin's sixteenth birthday, where they'd all had a ride in a horse and cart. April had loved it so much that Coral had promised to take her back the following year. Sadly she was taken by Bridger before they got the chance to make the trip.

'I want her to say her bye-byes in a horse and cart,' Coral said, firmly.

We'd received a donation from the Victim Support charity, which enabled us to plan a much more elaborate service than we'd ever have been able to afford ourselves. Knowing how much it would have meant to April, organising a horse and cart was the first thing we wanted to do, and we decided April's coffin would be carried in a white cart, drawn by two white horses wearing pink feathers. We would follow in a black car. Naturally we'd ask all of the mourners to wear pink.

Choosing April's coffin was a fresh agony in itself. At first, we thought about a pink coffin but, as we wanted pink flowers, we decided on white. We had so little of our daughter that we only needed a small casket, but seeing all the tiny boxes did nothing but remind us of how a parent should never have to bury their child. It was all so cruel.

Two days before the coroner's hearing, we met with Andy John and Hayley at the police station in Aberystwyth. We asked if it would be possible for some of the police officers who'd worked on the case to be pallbearers, but unfortunately Andy told us this wouldn't be possible due to police regulations.

On 16 September, which was a Monday, Dave picked us up at 8.30 a.m. Coral decided to wear pink trousers as a tribute to April. The hearing was an hour's drive away in Welshpool, so we picked up Hayley on the way. The proceedings were over almost as soon as they had begun. Andy spoke briefly about April's death, saying that, on the balance of probabilities, she had most likely died what he described as a 'violent death' in Mount Pleasant on 1 October 2012. It was merely a formality, and didn't tell us anything we didn't already know.

The coroner, Louise Hunt, was a nice lady who offered us her condolences on the loss of April. She explained to the court that she'd had to apply for special permission to hold an inquest in the absence of a body. Unfortunately the hearing would have to conclude without a verdict as to what caused April's death. The coroner told us that, without a body, she couldn't provide us with any information about how our daughter had died – at least nothing which hadn't been revealed during Bridger's trial. But perhaps, most importantly, she confirmed she could release April's remains to us and issue a death certificate.

A few days later, Coral and my mum went to the florists to sort out flowers for the service. Sunflowers were April's favourite, so they were an obvious choice. They let the florist decide the rest.

After they returned, we went with my mum to see the spot where April would be laid to rest, in the cemetery on the edge of Bryn-y-Gog. As it was an old graveyard, there were very few plots left and we were lucky to find a space for April there. We were relieved that one was available. It was comforting to know our little girl would be buried so close to the home where she'd been so happy.

'It was a sad and sombre moment,' I wrote in my diary that night. 'As the funeral grows close I just feel so low and down. I'm tearful all the time. It's so difficult. You get to the point where you just can't be bothered to do anything apart from mope and cry.'

The next day, the urn with April's remains was due to arrive at our house. We didn't have much of our daughter to bury, but we wanted her home one last time before she went on her final journey.

Coral recalls:

April's remains were due to arrive home on the Friday before the funeral, but the day got off to a bad start. I got up early to do some housework, as I thought the chores might distract me, but when I was clearing out the cupboards I found a little tracksuit I'd bought for April. We'd intended to give it to her for Christmas the year before, just a few months after she was taken, and she'd never had the chance to wear it. On this day of all days, it was too much to bear. I dissolved into tears and went straight back to bed.

Kath, the vicar, arrived at 3 p.m. with an urn containing the tiny pieces of ash and bone. It was all we had to show for our beautiful, vibrant little girl. Paul placed it tenderly on the mantelpiece and I didn't want to make a scene, so I waited until Kath had left before I removed it. Clutching it in my arms, I went straight back to bed. Tears rolled down my face as I lay there, cuddling all that was left of my little girl in my arms. I was barely aware of time passing and, before I knew it, I'd been lying in the same position for three hours. Later that evening, my friend Lesley came over to comfort me, but I was beyond consolation.

On the Saturday, I felt even worse. The post arrived and many people had sent us lovely cards and gifts ahead of the funeral. I was touched, but everything seemed to set me off. Just a quick glance at a picture of April would leave me sobbing uncontrollably and gasping for air.

I knew it was hard for Paul. All he could do was watch as I fell apart over and over again and I don't think the gravity of the situation had hit him yet. He seemed lost and numb. But for me, everything anyone did or said seemed to evoke another memory of the precious little girl we'd lost. As the funeral edged closer, it was all becoming so final.

In the afternoon, we had another visit from Kath. I couldn't even attempt to hold it together and I cried the whole way through it. She was very sympathetic, but she knew nothing she did could ease the pain that was slowly eating me up.

'I'm sorry,' I said, between sobs. 'I'm just so angry and I don't know how to make it stop.'

'The only thing I can say, Coral, is that it's better out than in,' Kath soothed.

'But she's gone,' I wept. 'She's gone and all I've got is a few bits of bone while he's alive in jail. Why did this happen to us?'

That evening, Jazz was very tearful, too. She usually kept her emotions to herself, so it always broke my heart to see her upset. We hugged and cried on the sofa for a long time and, when I woke up the next day, I felt slightly better.

On the Sunday, a few neighbours agreed to help us tend to April's Garden and that gave me something to focus on. The work was often too physical for me, although I was able to help with a bit of weeding and pruning. However, I still had a knot of dread in the pit of my stomach. Harley had been away for the weekend with a friend's family and we'd still to tell him that the funeral was to be the following Thursday. We'd wanted to get everything in place before we broke the news to him.

He arrived home around 4.30 p.m. and we spent a few hours

together, cuddled up on my bed watching television. It was so nice to spend some quality time with my son and the last thing I wanted to do was upset him, but I couldn't risk him hearing about the funeral at school or through a neighbour.

'Harley,' I said, with a deep breath. 'I've got something I need to talk to you about.'

'OK, Mum,' he replied. 'What is it?'

'On Thursday, we're going to be having a funeral for April,' I told him. I didn't think I had any tears left but soon we were both crying again. I tried to explain to Harley what would happen at the funeral, but I think he was too upset to take anything in. It just made everything so real. None of us were ready to say goodbye to April. We never would be.

Eventually, I calmed Harley down and we both went back downstairs but, as Paul tried to comfort me, I began to sob again. It wasn't long before I'd climbed back into bed, my arms wrapped tightly around the urn which I'd kept close to me ever since it had arrived two days previously. The undertaker had only wanted to give us a few days with April's remains but I flatly refused. I told him he had no choice but to let me keep them for as long as possible. Eventually it was agreed they'd be taken away on the Wednesday morning, the day before the funeral.

Having the remains in the house was strangely comforting and they helped me feel close to April, as I drifted off to sleep each night. On the Monday, Paul remarked that my mood had improved and admitted that over the weekend he'd been scared I wouldn't get to Thursday.

That day, Dave and Hayley took us to the undertakers,

where we met with Dilwyn and Kath to discuss final arrangements. Dave said the police would take care of closing the roads and controlling the crowd. He also offered to help with any last-minute preparations as he had a day off on the Wednesday, which was very kind of him.

On the Tuesday afternoon, the tears returned as it dawned on me that this was the last day I'd spend at home with April. It was rare for Paul and me to break down at the same time, but now we were both very emotional. I could see it slowly dawning on Paul what was about to happen. His calm facade had finally slipped. Desperate to spend as much time with April as possible, I took myself off to bed for a few hours in the afternoon, holding the urn tightly to me as ever.

Neither of us slept well that night. Dilwyn's secretary was due to call round just before 9 a.m. the next morning to collect the remains and we had to decide what items we wanted to place in April's coffin. In the end, we settled on a family photograph from our wedding, a sunflower made out of cloth, a teddy she'd had when she was young and one of her little scarves. Jazz had also bought matching necklaces, each with half a heart. One had the words 'little sister' inscribed on it and the other 'big sister'. With tears in her eyes, she placed one half with the rest of the items and fastened the other round her neck.

My friend Ceri knew how tough I would find Wednesday morning, so she arrived just before Dilwyn's secretary, as she wanted to support me. As we handed over the urn and the things we'd chosen for the coffin, I could barely stay upright. Ceri held me in her arms as I sobbed and sobbed.

'April,' I wailed. 'Why did he have to do this to you?'

Ceri was trying to keep her cool for my sake, but the tears were running down her cheeks as she tried to comfort me. Paul was crying too. Autumn was eerily silent and Storm was whimpering slightly. April had loved our dogs so much that they often slept in her bed. We found it adorable when she called them her 'darlings'. Sometimes, it seems animals have a sixth sense and it was like they knew what was happening. I wondered in that moment how we'd ever get through the next day.

Everything hit me like a ton of bricks when April's remains were taken back to the undertaker. While Ceri consoled Coral in the living room, I took myself off to the kitchen so I could cry alone. Coral had found these last few days extremely tough, perhaps even more trying than the court case. For that reason, I was trying my hardest to cry my own tears behind closed doors. I knew how much my wife needed me and I wanted so much to be strong for her.

After we'd all composed ourselves, Ceri suggested that she and Coral go into town to do a little shopping. I couldn't bear being in the house alone, so I took the dogs out for a long walk around Machynlleth. On the way back to the house, I stopped just a few yards from the cemetery and caught sight of the gravediggers working on the plot that had been earmarked for April. I suddenly felt sick and dizzy and I leaned against a tree to maintain my balance. It was a sight I hadn't been supposed to see.

The television cameras which had first congregated on the estate in the days after April vanished were beginning to reappear, one by one. I was almost oblivious. Shortly after I arrived home, it was time for Coral and me to visit April's coffin at the chapel of rest in the undertakers' offices.

Coral burst into tears immediately at the sight of April's coffin. Kath, who had taken us there, wrapped a supportive arm around her and comforted her before telling us that she'd leave us alone for a few minutes. As soon as she left, I saw a flash of anger in Coral's eyes and she began to scream.

'How could he do this?' she shrieked. 'Paul, how could he do this? How could he?' She spent a few minutes shouting and cursing Bridger before the anger subsided and she fell into my arms. Her sobs became quieter and quieter until they faded to a whimper. We sat there for around ten minutes, holding each other in silence, before we summoned the strength to leave.

Thursday 26 September dawned a grey and uninspiring day. Both Coral and I awoke before 7 a.m. I took the dogs for a walk and, as I passed the church, I noticed photographers and camera crews had already started to gather. Incredibly, no one noticed me. As I passed the White Lion pub, where Jazmin worked, I bumped into Coral's cousin, Frank, who had been staying there. He asked if he could join me on my walk. The service wasn't until noon, so we had a few hours to spare. I took him up the hill on the south side of the town where I'd spent many hours in reflection since April's death. The fresh air did us both good and I was home by 9 a.m.

By that point, friends and family were already gathered in the house. We'd decided that Dai, Fil, and Coral's dad, Tony, would carry April's coffin. I'd chosen not to be a pallbearer so I could walk behind the cortège with Coral, Jazmin and Harley as it left the church. One of Coral's other relatives was due to be the fourth pallbearer but he had fallen ill at the last minute and was unable to make the long journey to Machynlleth. Instinctively I asked Tracey to step in. She had already arrived at the house to support us, her pink bow pinned tenderly to her black dress. She'd been such a great friend to us over the past year that she seemed an obvious choice. Of course she agreed, but both Coral and I could tell she was nervous.

Friends, neighbours and family members slowly filed solemnly into the living room and I estimated that there must have been at least fifty people in the house. Our home hadn't been so full since that dreadful night almost a year beforehand, but it was touching to see many of the same faces. Our community was rallying round us yet again.

With a heavy heart, I popped upstairs and put on the clothes I'd picked for the occasion – a pink shirt and smart grey trousers. As ever, I fixed a pink bow onto my shirt above my top pocket. Coral was already dressed in a black and pink-striped top, black trousers and a bracelet with April's name on it. She was almost oblivious to our guests and was getting steadily more upset as the morning wore on. At one point, I thought I'd never be able to calm her down or stop her from shaking and crying. Eventually time got the better of us and Dilwyn arrived at the door. I was touched when I noticed he'd forsaken his usual black tie for a pink one, as had all of his staff.

A huge crowd of people had gathered on Bryn-y-Gog to see April's little white coffin and its horse-drawn carriage arrive out-side our house. Most were dressed in pink and some were clutching single red roses. Silence fell among our neighbours as

Coral, Harley and I slowly emerged. Some bowed their heads or dabbed their eyes. The only noise was the soft sound of the horses' feet on the ground. There were a few flashes, as some of the photographers who had congregated on the street tried to get a shot of us, but we barely noticed.

The coffin was inside a beautiful white glass hearse and beside it lay a pink wreath spelling out April's name. We walked slowly to the car and climbed in. Jazmin wanted to lead the mourners, who'd decided to go to the church on foot. She walked just behind our car, resplendent in a pink top, and our friends and neighbours began to follow respectfully behind.

When the door of the limousine closed, Coral really began to break down. Her sobs were breathless and she was verging on hysteria. Harley looked lost, but reached to hug his mum and kept his arms around her for the duration of the short journey. My own tears had begun to flow thick and fast as we edged closer to the church.

We got out of the car and there were cameras everywhere. Flashes were going off in every direction but I was crying so much I could barely see a thing. I couldn't believe how many mourners had gathered to pay their respects. The church was full to bursting and there were hundreds of people gathered outside, all wearing splashes of pink. As well as the police and mountain rescue teams, there were lots of civilian volunteers who'd assisted with the search in the first few days. I later discovered that one of the jurors from Bridger's trial had even come along to pay his respects. The service would be broadcast on speakers in the courtyard for those who couldn't gain entry to the church.

Kath came out to greet us and laid a supportive arm on Coral's shoulder. My wife's sobs had become quieter, but she was still visibly distressed.

The pallbearers carefully lifted April's coffin from the carriage and carried it into the church. Jazmin joined us at the entrance and her face was stained with tears. We followed slowly behind, my arm in Coral's and Jazmin's in Harley's.

As we walked to the front of the church behind the coffin, a montage of family pictures that Jazmin had made as part of a college project was playing on a large screen at the front of the church. It had been a real labour of love for our older daughter and she'd spent many painstaking hours making sure it looked perfect. It was a bittersweet moment. We looked so happy, blissfully unaware of the horrible fate that awaited us. Now, we'd never be a family of five again.

Jazmin had chosen the Emeli Sandé song, 'Read All About It Part Two' to play alongside the images. It was a song both she and April had liked. It played in the background as we made our way down the aisle. I heard several people in the congregation burst into tears as we passed and took our seats in the front row.

'There is nothing to express the grief, the shock, the pain, the emptiness, the anger, the despair which overwhelms us,' Kath began.

Coral's hand was still clasped to her face as she shook with silent sobs. I put my arm around her and tried to blink away my own tears.

'We honestly come before you asking for strength in time of darkness,' Kath went on. 'We have come together to remember April in the presence of God. We have come to celebrate her short life and grieve together, to say goodbye.

'Our hopes and dreams have changed because April has been taken from us. But we come also with a sense of thanksgiving for the many ways that April touched our lives and those with whom she came into contact.

'For a five-year-old she touched a great many lives. For Paul, Coral, Jazmin and Harley, April was and is extra special. But she touched us all and we think and feel differently because of the difference she made to us.

'Today, here in this place, she is linking us all together in grief. Yet, grief goes hand in hand with love. In whatever way we express our grief, it shows our love for April. And surely that is the most important thing for any human being of whatever age – simply to be loved.'

One of the parishioners, a local man named Jim Marshall, had written two poems about April in the week following her disappearance. We were so touched that he'd put so much time and effort into paying tribute to our little girl that we decided to have the poems as readings at the service. As April had adored school so much, we thought it was only fitting that they should be read by her teachers. The first, simply entitled 'April', was read by a class teacher called Sian Calban. The second, 'An Autumn Night', was read by the headteacher, Gwenfair Glyn.

We'd also chosen some hymns – 'All Things Bright and Beautiful', 'Oh Father On Your Love We Call' and 'Blessed Are The Pure In Heart'. We sang the last hymn in Welsh. I barely remembered anything about the service, apart from how beautiful the poems were. Before April's coffin was carried back out to the hearse, Kath said a few words of thanks on our behalf.

'We give thanks to God for all those who helped Paul and Coral in those darkest of days,' she said. 'The police, the search and rescue teams, the hundreds of volunteers, the people of this town and beyond.'

Both Coral and I were determined that something good should come of April's awful death and, a few days before the funeral, Coral decided that she'd like to sponsor a child in Africa in our daughter's name. With Kath's help, we did this through the charity World Vision and we held a collection at the back of the church as the mourners made their way out. Once again, the people of Machynlleth surpassed themselves and we raised £1250. The money was sent to the family of a five-year-old girl in Uganda. For a child living in one of the poorest countries in the world, this amount of money was truly life-changing. We later found out the donations enabled her parents to buy some land and a small shack, as well as a cow to give them a livelihood they could only have dreamed of before. In life, April was so loving and giving. It seemed appropriate that, in death, our daughter had granted another child the bright future she herself had been so cruelly deprived of.

It was only when we got outside that I really noticed how gorgeous the white horses were, with their pink feathers. I'd been so consumed by my tears as we left for the church that I hadn't taken a proper look at them.

The journey from the church to the graveyard was a fairly short one, so we walked behind the cortège in virtual silence, painfully aware that we were about to say our last goodbye. We were all very emotional when we arrived. The sobs of our friends and family were audible, as April's little casket was lowered into the ground. Then, Harley and Jazmin each let off a pink balloon before we all threw a single red rose on top of the coffin. We said a little prayer and held each other for a few moments in silence as, inwardly, we all said our final farewells. None of us wanted to leave. It felt so wrong leaving April there all alone.

After we'd composed ourselves, we made our way to the Celtica Visitor Centre. We mingled with all of our guests and it was lovely to see so many of the police officers who'd worked on the case.

'We'll never forget everything you've done for us,' I told Dave and Hayley, my voice choked with emotion.

By the time we arrived home at 3.30 p.m., Coral was wiped out. She lay on the sofa and fell asleep almost instantly, while I pottered around the house. I wasn't quite sure what to do with myself so, when darkness fell, I went for a short walk to the grave-yard with the dogs.

As April was buried so close to our house, I knew the temptation would be to visit her grave as often as I could. I had already decided that it wouldn't be healthy to spend every waking hour there, but I couldn't help visiting it that evening.

It was strangely comforting. Underneath the starlit sky, the graveyard was so quiet and peaceful and I felt a sense of calm come over me. It was lovely reading all the tributes to our little girl that had been laid there. One had a beautiful laminated picture of April and was signed simply from the 'Community of Carmarthenshire'.

'To the family of April,' it read. 'You will always be in our hearts and thoughts.'

I wiped a tear away and spent a few minutes kneeling quietly by the graveside before I managed to tear myself away. When I returned home, Coral was still in bed, so I reached for my diary.

'It's been so emotional today,' I wrote. 'I feel so tired and drained. This funeral has been hanging over us for so long. We weren't sure if we could have one. Coral and I desperately wanted one, so we could have a grave where we could visit April. It's a relief to now have a place where we can go to see her and I hope it puts Coral's mind at ease. It was hard to leave the graveyard when we did. I had to tear myself away, but I don't want to camp there.

'It was a sad but beautiful day for our April. Everyone was crying but they were all there for April and I find it helps me to know how many people have been touched by her. The kindness of people makes me cry sometimes. Jazz has picked up some of the local papers and from what they have written it seems like they have given April a lovely farewell.

'I'm OK – for me, April will always be with me in my memories and in my heart. I loved that girl and I miss her so much. I can't do anything for April but I can do something for Coral, Jazz and Harley by being there for them.

'I love you, April. Dad xxx.'

15

One Year On

Tuesday 1 October 2013 began in a very different way to Monday 1 October 2012. Then, I'd been restless the previous evening, anticipating the next day. It had been an unremarkable Sunday and we'd had little more to worry about than getting school uniforms organised for the week ahead. Now, it was almost unfathomable how we had no idea of how quickly, and how cruelly, our lives were about to change.

Coral went to bed early but I was restless, so I took Autumn and Storm on a late-night walk up the hill on the south side of Machynlleth, which had been my refuge for the past twelve months. It took much longer than usual, as I kept stopping and sitting down on the grass, thinking of April. But, no matter how tired and down I felt, I kept climbing until I reached the summit.

I still woke early the next day, but I had no April to gently coax from her bed. Coral didn't have to help her into her cerebral palsy suit or apply her eczema cream. The empty bed in the room our little girl had shared with her big sister seemed emptier than ever. But we had to go on.

As I prepared the morning coffee – Coral's, as always, with only a quarter of a teaspoon of coffee powder, three sugars and lots of milk – a solitary tear rolled down my cheek. My mornings seemed so empty without April in them. I tried to distract myself by taking long walks with the dogs, but really I wanted nothing more than to race April to the front gate before taking her to class. I could hear the children from the estate laughing and chatting as they made their way to school and it seemed so unfair that my little girl wasn't with them.

I found myself wondering what her school report would have been like this year. What new Welsh words would she have learned and what pictures would she have painted for her teachers?

As hard as it was, I managed to gather myself together when Coral came downstairs. I wanted to be strong for her, as I knew how much she'd struggled over the last week.

The days since the funeral had been quiet. On the Friday, Coral had stayed in bed for all but two hours. She only got up to go to the graveyard, where she and her friends tidied April's plot a little before heading home.

Shortly afterwards, Dave called round to drop off some of April's teddies. They'd been taken away as part of the initial DNA tests and I was beginning to worry we might never get them back. I was relieved to see them again. The passing of time had meant

April's scent had all but faded from them but as I held them close to me, it felt good to have them back where they belonged. It would be a painful process, but we'd decided we would eventually move April's teddies from her bed to a hammock we'd put up. It was unthinkable that we'd ever throw them out but we had to make some small changes to the room, for Jazmin's sake if nothing else. I couldn't imagine what it was like for her, as she drifted off every night, looking at the empty space where her sister had once slept.

Coral was very quiet over the weekend and seemed to hardly want to speak to anyone, even me. Since the funeral, she'd barely done anything but sleep. It made me feel anxious and stressed so I took the dogs for a long 15-mile walk in the hills to try and clear my head. I didn't realise that she'd been carefully writing a letter to Bridger, begging him to reveal what he'd done with the rest of April's remains.

Coral recalls:

After the funeral, everything made me feel sad and stressed. I just wanted to be alone. At times, I didn't even want to speak to Paul.

None of my family knew that I was writing to Bridger as I sat alone in my room. Paul had spent months putting his thoughts on paper but I'd never had the inclination, or the energy, to write much down.

It was only when I started to write that I realised how cathartic a process it was. I could feel my anger and grief bubbling to the surface, as my tears spilled onto the page. I wouldn't go as far as to say it felt good, but it was certainly a release of some sort. I'd never had the opportunity to properly put into words how I felt about the man who'd ripped our lives apart and how, in a final, cruel, insult, he hadn't even had the decency to admit to what really happened on that terrible night almost one year previously.

Don't get me wrong – I still had fantasies about hurting him. I hadn't stopped imagining what I'd do if he was stood in front of me and someone handed me the nail gun I'd been dreaming of while we sat just feet away from him in court. But, although I couldn't inflict physical pain on him, I wanted to make him suffer in some way. I hoped that giving him a tiny glimpse of the devastation he'd caused might go some way towards achieving my aim.

'Mark Bridger,' I wrote. 'It is a year since you took April from me and my family. Last week, I had to bury my daughter, which no mother should ever have to do, and, as I watched her coffin being lowered into the ground, the pain and anger I felt was truly unbearable.

'I cannot describe the hatred I have for you – it burns inside me each and every single day. You took my precious little girl from me and destroyed my family. You have torn my whole life to pieces. I'm now asking you to tell me where her body is. As a parent yourself, you should understand the bond you have with your children.

'If you have any decency, I ask that you find it within yourself to tell me where you put April. We buried what we have of April, but the rest of her is out there somewhere. I will not be able to rest until we can bury all of her, so find it within yourself to tell me what you did with her. If there is a shred of humanity left inside of you, then find it in your heart to tell us where our baby girl April is.

'Coral Jones.'

I read and re-read my letter many times. It was just a snapshot of how Bridger had made me feel because, in truth, there weren't enough words in the English language to accurately describe how much my life had been shattered by his actions.

After much deliberation, I decided not to send it. Of course, I was almost positive he wouldn't reply, even if I did send it, but I was a broken woman and I didn't have the strength to enter a dialogue with him on the off-chance he decided to respond. I didn't want to face him while I was a shell of the person I was before April disappeared. That could wait.

The day before our little girl's first anniversary, I took my letter to Paul and explained what I'd been doing. He took some paper clips and fastened it to a page in his diary in case I changed my mind.

I didn't hold out much hope that Bridger would pay any attention to the questions I longed to have answered, but I knew one day I'd find the strength to ask them. That day just wasn't today.

Throughout the day, presents arrived from friends, neighbours and even strangers. We were so touched by how many people were thinking of us on April's first anniversary. Among the gifts was a star named after April and a map of the sky so we could find it. This made us both emotional and Coral had a little cry. It was like our beautiful daughter would always be looking down on us.

Someone else had paid to have April's name put on an Eddie Stobart truck.

Although all of our family and friends had made the journey to be with us the previous week, many felt compelled to return for April's first anniversary. My mum and Dai made the journey down from New Quay and Sue came from Holyhead. It was nice to have them around us, as it was important for us to mark the day with some of the people who'd loved April most.

The afternoon was fairly quiet. Coral and some of her friends went to the graveside, while I stayed at home. I found that my mind constantly flashed back to the same day one year ago. Coral and I had been so carefree, as we wandered round the shops in Aberystwyth, mulling over which television to buy for Harley. I wondered how we would have reacted if someone had told us that these would be our last few hours of normality; how we would have felt if we'd known that soon the anonymity of our simple lives would be shattered forever. The things that we worried about before the night of 1 October 2012 now seemed so trivial. I'd never stop wishing that we could turn back the clock.

Coral had decided she wanted to release some Chinese lanterns on Bryn-y-Gog in the evening. The lanterns had brought us comfort when we first released them the week after April was taken and we knew how much she would have loved them. We announced our plans on Facebook and over a hundred people came to the estate. Some also brought pink balloons. Those who had been touched by our story but lived too far away to attend sent us messages saying they would hold their own memorials and, soon, lantern releases were planned as far afield as Southport,

Bristol and Blackpool. Some others simply pledged to light a candle in our daughter's name.

I'd written in my diary that there were times I wondered if the people of Machynlleth would one day forget about us and what we'd been through but when I stepped out of the house and saw so many people gathered on the grass, I knew April would be in the hearts of the people of our small town forever.

We let the lanterns off around 6 p.m. The sun was setting and they looked beautiful as they soared into the salmon-tinted sky. I fully expected to feel low and tearful, so I was surprised to find the whole experience rather uplifting.

Thanks to the actions of one evil man, our quiet town would never be the same again. When he'd driven off with April in his car that horrendous night one year ago, Bridger had taken away the light of our lives. The darkness of that evening would live with us forever, no matter how many lanterns we lit. But Bridger could never take away the community spirit of Machynlleth – it was the glue that had held the town together during the night-mare no one could have foretold. Together we were far stronger than he'd ever be.

There were so many people gathered outside that Coral, Jazmin and I were outside the front of the house until 8.30 p.m. chatting to them. A few of Harley's friends had come along, so he was happy to play with them as we mingled. Exactly twelve months ago, many of these people had stood outside our front door, similarly desperate to lend their support. But then the mood was one of panic and distress. Now the atmosphere was much calmer. It was a time for reflection.

It was helpful that we weren't stuck inside alone, replaying every minute of what had happened a year previously. We'd gone over our last conversations with April hundreds of times but, no matter how many hours we spent agonising over each tiny detail, nothing would ever change. With the help of our counsellors, we were slowly getting our heads around this.

We also posed for pictures for the local press. We were happy to cooperate with their request for a story. The coverage of April's funeral had by its nature been very sad, so we hoped that this news might be something a little bit more positive for people to read.

By 9 p.m., most of the visitors had drifted away and Coral was exhausted. She spent an hour unwinding in front of the TV before going to bed. As usual, I didn't feel as tired, so I took Autumn and Storm out for a while.

As I walked, I thought about the week ahead and I knew it too would be difficult. Our friends and neighbours couldn't be with us every hour of every day and I appreciated that there would be times when both Coral and I would replay some of the worst moments of those initial, terrible days: the first visit from Andy John when he told us about Bridger's claims he'd run April over; Coral's agony as she addressed the nation's press; being taken to the sanctuary for the first time to be told about the forensic evidence and, of course, the moment we were told Bridger had been charged with murdering our little girl.

But, as I returned home to write in my diary, I realised all of that could wait. For now, I was just glad that we'd got through the day.

'Today turned out to be a bit more of a happy event than a sad one,' I wrote. 'It's strange, but we were celebrating April's life rather than mourning the fact she's been away from us for one year, lost to that monster Mark Bridger. It was a good night – it wasn't full of pain and anger with people being sad and crying. It was more cheerful and I felt better for having family and friends around me. All in all, that horrible day turned out to be better than we expected thanks to our family, friends and neighbours and everyone on the Bryn-y-Gog estate.

'I love you, April. Dad xxx.'

16

Neverending Battles

As our first year without April ended, Machynlleth slowly began to get back to some sort of normality. Our daughter's death meant our little town would never be the same again. However, slowly but surely, the local people tentatively began their attempt to pick up the pieces of a world that had been shattered beyond comprehension.

The visits from the television cameras and newspaper reporters slowed to the extent that they became infrequent. We still took the occasional phone call from the media about the campaign, and we were happy to give any interviews which might help our cause. Now, however, things were much more on our terms. The press would never again camp out on Bryn-y-Gog en masse or try to sneak pictures of us as we left the house. The headlines had changed and other tragedies had begun to fill the column inches.

Gradually more and more children started to appear on Bryn-y-Gog in the evenings. For months, their parents hadn't let them wander far from the front door, terrified of what might happen if they lost sight of them for just a second. But, in time, the same parents began to rationalise what had happened. The odds against another child being taken were so slim as to be almost impossible. If we all lived in fear, we'd be letting the evil that led to April's abduction claim another victory. Coral and I were glad these children were being allowed to run around on the estate, chasing after each other on their bikes after the school day had finished.

But while a sense of routine returned to most lives in town, our pain didn't lessen as time went on. All we could do was attempt to live with it.

Even though April was gone, some of her friends still called round from time to time. Their visits were bittersweet for Coral and me. On the one hand, we revelled in their childlike innocence. They didn't tiptoe around us and they talked unreservedly about April, so it was lovely to see how fondly our daughter was remembered by the other children on the estate, but it was also a stark reminder of what we'd lost.

'Do you know I'm six now?' Louise, one of the girls who had played with April on the night she vanished, asked, as she sat in our back garden one afternoon. I had to swallow hard to stop a lump forming in my throat. April never saw her sixth birthday; neither would she see her seventh, eighth or any birthday ever again. Yet we'd watch Louise and the rest of her peers grow into young women, getting their first jobs and bringing home their first boyfriends, perhaps one day becoming mothers themselves. The pain was indescribable.

Amy had always been fairly shy, but she still smiled and waved to us on the estate. We could only hope that she hadn't been too affected by the horror of what she'd witnessed. Only time will truly tell.

Some of April's friends asked where her pink bike was. It was understandable, as she never went out to play without it, but this also made me tearful. Almost as soon as April had gone missing, the police had removed her bike for examination by the forensic teams, and later by scientists such as Roderick Stewart. It was key to dismantling Bridger's defence, as the various experts who looked at it were able to conclude that the bike hadn't been involved in a collision with a car, as Bridger had claimed. After the trial, Dave and Hayley had told us that we could have the bike back if we wanted. Coral and I weren't sure what to do, but in the end we told the police to keep it. Having it in the house would be a permanent reminder of that awful night and it was more than we could bear.

We tentatively began clearing out some of April's toys, putting them in bags to send to charity shops where we hoped they'd go to other children who'd love them as much as she had. There were some things we couldn't bear to let go of, however, like a little Jack and Jill house she'd played with for hours on end. We also kept her first bike. For me, it held such precious memories of the many hours I'd spent on the grass outside our house, teaching her to ride it. Unlike her second bike, it wasn't tainted by the nightmare that was October 2012. Every time I looked at it, I remembered the look of sheer determination I'd seen in those big, brown eyes, that fighting spirit she'd inherited from her mum.

At times, the hole in our lives seemed so huge that Coral and I even discussed trying for a fourth child. Coral thought it might give us a focus, something besides our grief to concentrate on. But we soon decided this was not a good idea. We were both in our forties and I quickly calculated that, even if we managed to conceive within the year, I'd be approaching sixty-five by the time the baby was Jazmin's age. After all we'd been through we just didn't have the energy for more sleepless nights. Besides, April had been our world. Because of our various health problems, we'd devoted so much of our time to caring for her, as we'd been unable to work. There was no doubt that we'd love another child with all our hearts, but it would be so hard not to draw comparisons with the little girl we'd lost, and that wasn't fair on anyone.

Behind closed doors, we also still wrestled with the agony of not knowing exactly what had happened to April. This was something we'd never fully come to terms with. One evening in early November, Coral disappeared in the car and texted to say she was at Bridger's old house in Ceinws. Delirious with anguish, she'd gone to find the rest of April's remains. After some persuasion, I managed to calm her down and she returned home a short while later. It was hard to think about things logically, but if the highly trained, professional search teams had found nothing after seven months of searching, there was very little chance of us having any success.

A few days later, it was Jazmin's eighteenth birthday. We tried our very best to make this a happy occasion. I put up banners and balloons and Coral invited friends over for a party. Jazmin seemed to have fun and even Coral and I found ourselves enjoying the day.

Still, April was always at the forefront of our minds, and the next day we felt crushed knowing she hadn't been there to celebrate with us.

As we struggled with our personal demons, we still had a very public battle to fight. Neither Coral nor I was prepared to give up on our fight against child pornography. The need to devote greater resources to policing the internet was only hammered home more when someone claiming to be Bridger appeared on a Facebook site we'd made in April's name, leaving comments and 'liking' our updates.

At first, we were terrified he'd managed to gain access to the sites whilst in prison and was taunting us from behind bars. We spoke to Dave, who investigated on our behalf and concluded that the most likely explanation was that the comments had been made by online trolls pretending to be our daughter's killer. How anyone could think this was appropriate or acceptable we'll never know, but we'd come to realise that there were a lot of things about the human race that we'd never truly understand.

On 18 November 2013, we did have a bit of a breakthrough. Government ministers had held a summit with some of the major internet companies, who agreed to a number of measures which would hopefully reduce child abuse online.

We received a phone call from Claire Perry that morning to advise us of some of the changes that had been implemented by these companies. Google and Microsoft both had agreed to make changes to their search engines to help prevent paedophiles from accessing videos or images depicting child abuse.

Eric Schmidt, executive chairman of Google, told the government that his firm had taken steps to prevent child abuse images being returned from over 100,000 unique search terms. The changes were to be rolled out in 159 different languages over a six-month period, meaning paedophiles all over the world would be targeted.

Microsoft chief executive Steve Ballmer said his company had taken advice on blacklist search terms from the National Crime Agency and banned all child abuse images, videos and pathways from these keywords.

Both companies had agreed, as we had suggested, to display clear warning messages to people who used any of the blacklisted search terms, telling them of the consequences of their actions and redirecting them to the pages of charities set up to help prevent the sexual abuse of children.

Together, Microsoft and Google accounted for around 95 per cent of the searches made on the internet, so this was definitely a step in the right direction and proof that our hard work had, at least in part, paid off. David Cameron called this 'huge progress'.

However, we couldn't help but feel it wasn't quite enough. It had taken the deaths of April and Tia Sharp to prompt these companies into taking action and we'd really hoped for legislation to underpin these changes. Without a proper legal and financial deterrent we feared – and still do fear – that images and videos would slip through the cracks. How many more children would have to be abused or killed before the government would really crack down on the companies allowing people to access these images?

Coral, Jazmin and I decided to give an interview to Channel 5 News later that night. It was the first time we had allowed Jazmin to appear on television with us, but now she was eighteen, we felt she was capable of making her own decision about media appearances.

'These companies could have stepped up a little earlier,' I said. 'I'm not saying it would have saved April but it would definitely slow paedophiles down. We do need a group, a unit, that will go out there and search these people out.'

'I'm happy the government is starting to take action,' Coral added. 'But I don't think it's enough.'

Jazmin had been shocked when she'd found an explicit picture on one of the Facebook pages we'd created in April's memory. As a young person who had grown up in the digital age, she perhaps understood the perils of the internet even more than we did.

'I don't think the internet is a safe place at all,' she admitted. 'You can't trust anything that's on there and you've got to be really, really careful especially with Facebook and YouTube and things like that. It's not a safe place for children to be at all.'

'It's good that the Prime Minister and the internet providers are now acting on the public's wishes,' I wrote in my diary that night. 'It's a shame that kids have to be murdered and raped before anyone takes any notice. There were people out there saying this needed to be addressed years ago – it was a disaster waiting to happen.

'I love you, April. Dad xxx.'

The following week, we were invited to London to a special awards ceremony organised by *Best* magazine to honour Britain's bravest women. Coral had been nominated on account of the campaign.

The train journey to Birmingham from Machynlleth was a little fraught. There were only two carriages, which were extremely crowded, and this made Coral anxious. Thankfully our connection to Euston was far more comfortable and when we arrived we were taken by taxi to a very nice four-star hotel in Central London called the Crowne Plaza.

The magazine gave us a chaperone called Tracey, who couldn't do enough for us – so much so I nicknamed her *seren bach*, Welsh for 'little star'. Coral was one of nine women who had been nominated for an award and she was truly humbled to be included. All of the women had unique and inspirational stories. One woman, Jane Plume, had been left devastated after her best friend Gina had been tragically killed in a car accident. Shortly afterwards, Gina's husband Shaun had died of cancer and Jane had taken in their two sons, Lewis and Ashton. Another winner, Jane Gates, had built a holiday home for seriously ill children because it was the last thing her nine-year-old son Sebastian had asked her to do before he succumbed to a rare form of childhood cancer.

The evening before the awards, we were all taken to a performance of the West End musical *Dirty Dancing*. We had some of the best seats in the house and we were treated like royalty. Coral bonded quickly with all of the other women and it was really nice to see her enjoying herself for once.

The next day all of the winners were treated to a makeover before the ceremony. I couldn't believe my eyes when Coral emerged in a gorgeous purple designer dress, with styled hair and perfect make-up. She looked so stunning she almost took my breath away. For the first time in over a year, I saw the woman I'd fallen in love with – but not just because she so looked so beautiful. As I watched her laughing and joking with the other girls I saw just a tiny hint of the sparkle that had been missing from her eyes for a long, long time.

The awards themselves were held in a private residence at Buckingham Gate, located in a swish part of London that is home to many international embassies. The evening was to be hosted by television presenters Ruth Langsford and Eamonn Holmes. I lost count of how many celebrities we saw. It was a little surreal when we were sat at a table next to Coleen Nolan and her husband, Ray, but throughout the night one thing was made very clear: the real stars were the ordinary women whom everyone had come to honour.

It took an hour and a half to give out all of the awards and each of the women made a short speech. I accompanied Coral to collect hers and she managed to say a few words about the campaign, which was very brave and made me incredibly proud. We were both in tears as we listened to all of the other winners speak. Everyone had overcome unbelievable adversity to get to where they were and it was an honour to be invited to sit amongst them.

That evening I let Coral rest while I wrote in my diary, which I'd brought along in my suitcase.

'Tonight I was so emotional listening to everyone's stories,' I said. 'I cried most of the evening at the various things that were said – what a softie. But it was great to see Coral relax and beam with a big smile. This did remind me of April.

'I love you, April. Dad xxx.'

*

In the months after April's death, local people had begun raising money in April's name through various fundraising activities. Some of this money would be distributed to nearby charities but they also wanted to give us a donation for a family holiday, given everything we'd been through.

We decided that we would use these funds to visit Coral's brother, Ian, and his wife, Carol, in Adelaide, South Australia. Ian and Carol had emigrated in 2007, shortly after April was born, and hadn't seen her since she was baby. However, Coral and Ian were very close and regularly kept in touch on Skype and Facebook.

We made the difficult decision to travel to Australia for Christmas and New Year. Both Coral and I felt a pang of sadness and couldn't shake the feeling that we were leaving April behind, as we wouldn't be there to tend to her grave on Christmas Day. But the memories of the awful, empty Christmas of 2012 came flooding back and we realised we weren't quite ready to face another festive season in our little home if April wasn't in it.

We left Machynlleth on Monday 9 December. My mum and Dai gave us a lift to Manchester Airport, as Dai's van could accommodate all of our luggage. From there we flew to Dubai where we caught our connection to Australia.

More than twenty-four hours later, Ian met us at Adelaide Airport. It was a very emotional reunion for him and Coral and there were a lot of tears. It was only then that I realised how difficult things must have been for Ian and Carol, being stuck on the other side of the world while their family went through the worst trauma imaginable. They must have felt so lost and helpless. While Carol liked to talk about April and share memories of her, Ian found this very difficult.

They were fantastic hosts and took us on lots of exciting trips. Harley, in particular, was captivated by the kangaroos and wallabies. Ian also took Harley and me on a fishing trip to Lake Alexandrina, which lies around sixty miles south-east of Adelaide. Harley was over the moon when he caught the first fish, a carp weighing almost 10lb. Both Ian and I were in hysterics as he started wiggling his bum and doing a little dance in celebration. It was the happiest I'd seen him in months. We went on to catch thirty-four different fish that day and, by the end of the trip, Harley was so full of excitement that he was speaking so fast we could hardly understand a word he was saying. As soon as he got home to Machynlleth, he began putting coins in a piggy bank and told us he was saving to go back.

However, while we were in Australia we also got a call from Hayley, who told us that Bridger planned to appeal against his whole life sentence.

Coral recalls:
When Hayley's number flashed up on my phone I felt that familiar sense of dread grip me. I knew she wouldn't trouble us on holiday unless it was absolutely necessary but I didn't know why she would be calling.

'I'm so sorry to interrupt your break, Coral,' she said. 'But we didn't want you to see this in the newspapers.'

She explained that Bridger had launched an appeal against the whole life term handed out. It was almost too much to bear, especially when we heard he'd be given £20,000 in legal aid to do so. His legal bills had already cost the taxpayer £150,000 and I was at a loss as to why honest, hardworking people were continually being forced to foot the bill for his lies.

'It's like he wants to torture us even more,' Paul sighed, when I relayed the news to him. 'He's always got the upper hand.'

Hayley had explained that an initial hearing on Bridger's sentence would take place at the Court of Appeal in London in January, a few days after we got back from our holiday. Both Paul and I were determined we wanted to attend. If Bridger was going to put us through the mill, then he was going to have to face us while he did so.

I tried not to let the news put a dampener on our time in Australia. I was determined to give Jazmin and Harley the best Christmas I possibly could, as last year's had been so awful. I'd always dreamed of visiting Ian and Carol, but I'd never dreamed we'd be here without April.

It was lovely to see my brother, but I could see how much he was hurting about April. The pain was evident in his eyes. He was obviously at a very different point in the grieving process from the rest of us, having been separated from us all while the nightmare unfolded.

Christmas Day was very different from usual. Carol cooked a beautiful meal but we ate it outside in the sunshine, under a marquee in the garden.

It was while we were in Australia that I began doing some of my own writing. I didn't have a diary like Paul, but the letter I'd written to Bridger had shown me how much of a relief it was to get my thoughts down on paper.

'It feels so wrong not having my little April here with us,' I wrote, tears stinging my eyes. 'Her Uncle Ian can't speak about it as it hurts him so much. It doesn't feel like Christmas without my baby girl. We were all supposed to come to Australia together but I've brought her here in my heart.

'I wish I could change places with April. I've lived so much of my life. I've had three lovely children who mean the world to me. But I have to go on, for the sake of my other children.'

We arrived home on 7 January, fatigued and jet-lagged and already dreading our long journey to the Court of Appeal in London. We were relieved when we received a call from Hayley a few days later, telling us that we wouldn't have to make the trip after all: Bridger had abandoned the appeal against his whole life tariff. Still, we were angry that he'd been allowed to put us through the mill and place us under even more strain during what was always going to be a stressful time of year. It was like we'd never be free of his sick games.

'That bastard can rot slowly in misery and fear for the rest of his life,' I wrote. 'It's not much comfort for us, but a huge weight off our minds knowing he'll never be released.'

Shortly after Bridger dropped his appeal, we were contacted by a charity called Missing People. In partnership with the National Crime Agency, Missing People helps operate the Child Rescue Alert system. Although the alert issued in the immediate aftermath of April's disappearance sadly didn't produce the results we'd hoped for, we still passionately believed it could save the life of another child.

Jo Youle, the charity's Chief Executive, explained to us that the Child Rescue Alert system was to be extended to directly involve members of the public. Previously, appeals were circulated largely via the media but now people were being asked to sign up to receive alerts to their mobile phones.

In short, if a suspected abduction occurred in a certain area, everyone who had signed up to receive the alert would receive a text containing as much information as possible about the incident. This might include a photograph of the child or, if appropriate, a description of the vehicle in which they had been taken.

Coral and I understand better than most people that, when your child goes missing, all you want is for everyone around you to look for them. When Missing People invited us to London to help promote the re-launch of the scheme, we were happy to attend.

Coral took part in a photocall at King's Cross Station before we were taken to the House of Lords for a civic reception hosted by the Home Secretary, Theresa May. The following day, we also visited the Missing People headquarters in South London, where we were given a chance to see first-hand the amazing work the charity and its many volunteers do every day on behalf of families like ours.

Since then, we have attended several fundraising events organised by them and we hope to have a productive relationship with them for many years to come. Working together, perhaps we can ensure another family's story does not have as tragic an ending as ours.

As 2014 progressed, we realised we had to adjust to our new lives as best we could. My diary entries soon became so infrequent to the point where now they've almost stopped completely.

When we visited Bridger's house, it became apparent to both of us that we'd never get closure. Now it seems almost ridiculous that we thought closure was even achievable. We feel April's absence every day, as keenly as we felt it on that awful autumn evening when she was first taken.

What we are slowly learning to do is live with the pain. We're gradually coming to realise that some days will be worse than others, and that we have to accept the bad days are now part of our lives. It would be easy to wish our suffering was over, and that we were no longer here, but we don't just have April to think of. We have two other beautiful children who have shown courage and strength beyond their years throughout this whole, terrible trauma. Jazmin and Harley need us and we have to keep going for them, if nothing else.

On our good days we can achieve a lot, much more than we would ever have imagined. We still occasionally make the long journey from Machynlleth to London to meet politicians and charity executives in a bid to stop this nightmare from happening to another family.

One of the reasons I fell in love with Coral when I first met her fifteen years ago was her fire and determination. Once she puts her mind to something, there's no stopping her. Even Mark Bridger and his unspeakable acts of evil have not been able to extinguish this fire, not completely. This is how I know that she won't rest until the government makes a legal commitment to ban search engines from returning results showing child pornography.

It was only when we were gathering together our notes in preparation for writing this book that I had the chance to read what Coral had written while we were in Australia. It brought tears to my eyes, but the tears were not solely those of sadness. I was also crying with pride. Because, despite everything that has been thrown at our family, it has remained intact. Bridger may have taken away the light of our lives, but he hasn't been able to break us. Against what at times seemed like insurmountable odds, we have remained as one tight-knit unit.

'This is just the start of our fight,' read the words on the page, in my wife's handwriting. 'Goodnight, our baby girl, April Sue-Lyn Jones. You will always be our hearts. We love you.

'Mum and Dad xxx.'

Acknowledgements

Since April was taken from us, the support we've received from friends and strangers alike has been overwhelming. To mention them all by name would probably merit a book in itself, but there are a few people we'd like to recognise.

Writing April's story has been an emotional and often draining process, but we felt it was important that it was told by the two people who knew and loved her best – her mum and dad. We'd like to thank Kerri Sharp, our editor at Simon & Schuster UK, for allowing us the opportunity to do this. We'd also like to thank our agent Clare Hulton and Jack Falber of Medavia for their role in making this possible. We are grateful, too, to Graham Ogilvy of Scottish News Agency for his advice in the initial stages of this process.

Many others have given freely of their time to read the various drafts of this manuscript, especially Helen O'Brien, Danielle Hoffman and Chantelle Rees, and we'd like to thank them for their input.

Special thanks must go to the ordinary people of Machynlleth, for their unwavering support since the awful night of 1 October 2012. We are indebted to every single person who tried to ease our suffering in some way, even through the smallest of gestures. We often say that the townspeople formed a 'ring of steel' around us in our weakest moments and we could not have survived this ordeal without them.

We'd also like to express our gratitude to everyone who helped look for April – from the civilian volunteers who travelled from all corners of the country to join the search party in the first few days after her disappearance, to the highly skilled teams who braved the elements to comb the vast and varied terrain of mid-Wales for six long months. We will never forget what they have done for us.

We are, of course, forever in the debt of everyone who helped bring Mark Bridger to justice, rightfully ensuring that he will never have the freedom to hurt another child again. In particular, we'd like to thank Elwen Evans QC and everyone from the Crown Prosecution Service who worked on the case, as well as the extremely dedicated officers from Dyfed-Powys Police and their colleagues from other forces who assisted them in this investigation. A special mention is reserved for our family liaison officers, Dave Roberts and Hayley Heard. Both have been towers of strength for us and our family and we will remember their kindness and professionalism for the rest of our lives.

Last but not least, we wish to thank our family and close

ACKNOWLEDGEMENTS

friends. Their unconditional love and support has given us the strength to go on when the burden of our loss seemed too much to bear. Despite their own grief for April, they have always been there for us. But, above all, we'd like to thank our amazing children, Jazmin and Harley, whose bravery and resilience astounds us every day.

missing people

Registered Charity No. 1020419

Missing People is an independent charity, which offers a lifeline when someone disappears. You can call or text 116 000 for advice, support and options if you, or someone you love, goes missing or runs away — it's free, 24 hour and confidential.

284 Upper Richmond Road West
London SW14 7JE
Tel: 020 8392 4590
www.missingpeople.org.uk

You can help support Missing People by texting HOPE to 70707 now and give £3 to Missing People. Your gift could help bring a missing child home. Text costs £3 plus network charge. Missing People receives 100 per cent of your donation. Obtain bill payer's permission. Missing People may contact you in the future to update you on their work.

Customer care 08448 479800. Charity No 1020419.

April Jones Trust

http://www.youcaring.com/nonprofits/
april-jones-trust-/183528

April Jones Trust is set up by Coral and Paul Jones to
commemorate their daughter and help other children in need,
schools, youth clubs and other such worthy causes.

Coral and Paul Jones are tirelessly campaigning for a change in
the images you can find on the internet and want a law against
people putting these indecent images on the net. April's killer had
accessed indecent images before she was so cruelly taken away.

There are two ways you can help this fundraiser -

- **To kindly donate money to April Jones Trust at the
  web address above**
- **To sign the April's Law petition at
  www.gopetition.com/petitions/aprils-law-uk.html
  and kindly share it with others and on your social networks**

Thank you everyone for supporting and donating to this special fundraiser

APRIL'S LAW 100%